THE BIG REVEAL

KEYS TO BUILDING YOUR **DREAM HOME**
AND YOUR **DREAM MARRIAGE**

ALISON CREWS

publish@cbpteam.com
www.CEOBookPublishing.com

Ordering Information:

Quantity sales. Special discounts are available on quantity purchases by corporations, associations, and others. For details, contact the publisher at the address above.

Orders by U.S. trade bookstores and wholesalers. Please contact Tel: (813) 970-8470 or visit www.CEOBookPublishing.com

Printed in the United States of America First Printing 2025

ISBN Paperback: 979-8-9927710-2-2
ISBN Hardcover: 979-8-9927710-3-9

Bible Scriptures are taken from the New International Version (NIV) and the English Standard Version (ESV)

Dedication

This book is dedicated to my beloved husband Bovell and my darling daughter Abigail. Thank you for your unconditional love, encouragement and support. My heart is full. It is said that home is where the heart is. I thank God that wherever we are, I am HOME!

— Alison Crews

"The ache for home lives in all of us,
the safe place where we can go as we are
and not be questioned."
— Maya Angelou

Contents

Introduction

What is "home?" The answer depends more on who you ask than on any universally agreed upon answer. It's not like asking what *Pi* is or even what water is. Even the definition of a "house" is more concrete and certain than the notion of "home." For example, home for me is the place where I find myself naked (nude as well as vulnerable) the greatest number of times and afraid the least number of times. It is the place where I feel both loved and accepted in all the different ways that I am and will be. Home is unconditional. It is the place that I can always return to. Home is a place of peaceful familiarity that I miss when I am away too long. If I can't be naked there without feeling anxious or afraid, then I most certainly would not call that place "home." It would simply be the place in which I reside.

Over the years, home ownership rates in the US have varied widely based on a lot of factors, including socioeconomic, generational and cultural aspects. However, despite when, where, or how you categorize the buyer, they all have one thing in common: the feeling that buying a home represents both the promise and the evidence of what is possible. It is one of those payoffs people talk about when sharing anecdotes about hard work. It also does not matter who you are, where you come from, whether you feel that the odds are stacked against you or are mostly in your favor, purchasing a place to call home shows the world that you have made it, that you are officially "adulting," and that you have reached at least one of the universal measures of success.

What does your *dream house* look like? I do not know anyone who hasn't asked themselves that question. Even as a little kid, I remember daydreaming about the kind of house I would live in one day. The preoccupation with pursuing one's *dream house* is embedded in our culture. Look at how buying a home is a goal or milestone in popular board games. If you have ever played "Monopoly" or "The Game of Life," you know that buying a home or other property pushes you closer toward winning. Even toys like the iconic Barbie have a "Dream House." Much like with board games and toys, those who can buy their dream house are always described as having made it. They are *#winning*.

Look at the popularity of reality TV shows that deal with real estate, home improvement, home remodeling, celebrity homes, tiny homes, vacation homes, homes on boats, homes on wheels, home makeovers, and even community home makeovers. They all reflect how important home ownership is within our society. Our appetite, attitude, and appreciation for home ownership are all important to consider before pressing toward that goal. A funny thing happened when I took my own advice and reflected on some of those things for myself. I began to realize just how many parallels there were between the journey toward owning my dream house and my journey toward my dream relationship, which for me is marriage. For example, I discovered that the type of house that I wanted for myself totally aligned with the type of husband I wanted for myself. Also, my attitude and appreciation for home ownership mapped perfectly to my attitude and appreciation for marriage. Recognizing this unexpected correlation is what compelled me to write down and explore these parallels with others in the hope that someone will find it as interesting as I do and maybe even helpful in some way.

- 1 -

Reflections in the Review

It is often said that you need to look backward before moving forward, or at least that is what I was taught in my high school driver's ed class. Since the early 1900s, a "small adjustable warning mirror for automobiles" was installed in vehicles so that the driver could see the road behind them. This same "rearview mirror" has also become a popular metaphor for the wisdom found in past life lessons. Warren Buffet, American businessman, investor, and philanthropist, says, "In the business world, the rearview mirror is always clearer than the windshield." I agree with Mr. Buffet, but I also know that the windshield is much bigger for a reason. What is ahead of us is always bigger, greater, and, in some ways, scarier than what is behind us. However, both points of view are necessary to help us safely get to wherever we are going.

That said, I want to reflect on the word "home" for a moment. It can mean different things to different people, depending on life experiences. This is why, when looking to buy, remodel, or even build a new home, there are endless possibilities for features, layouts, and other design elements. Before making these decisions, a good first step, believe it or not, is to look back at your childhood for clues as to what you may like or might not like about your future home. As you look back, things like the curb appeal, total square footage, or the function and style of each room must all be carefully considered. Your childhood home (the good, the bad, or the ugly) and your feelings about it have the most influence on your current home preferences. Do you like modern, traditional, craftsman, colonial, brick, stucco, multilevel, split-level, or single-story? Is your preferred location rural, city, suburbs, or near the coast? Am I suggesting that you spend time thinking about the place you grew up in before deciding where you want to live now? YES, that is precisely what I am saying. If you do not force yourself to identify your preferences and thoroughly explore the emotions that are connected to your ideas about "home," then you could end up investing hundreds of thousands of dollars only to find yourself miserable, either because your new home lacks something that you didn't realize you needed or because your new home brings up negative feelings associated with your past.

I hope this does not sound like some weird psychoanalytic *mumbo jumbo*, especially since they don't exactly cover this sort of thing in the "Home Buying" guides or workshops you may have encountered. Can you imagine, after scheduling a consultation with your realtor or builder, that instead of talking about location, budget, or the "must haves" for your new home, they instead guided you through an exercise of connecting to your *inner child* and recalling memories that you associate with home? "*Say what now? Come again?*" My husband would have given that suggestion a firm "*No, Ma'am. No, thank you!*" I imagine very few people would immediately jump on board with this idea. However, the truth is that reflecting on your childhood memories of home will always provide valuable insights that could save you a lot of time, money, and emotional distress. Let me share some of my insights from doing this little exercise for myself.

Children are small, and so the world around them seems very big in comparison. Almost everything and everyone I remember during that time of my life seemed bigger, taller, stronger, prettier, and sometimes even smarter, but not ever any better than me. I remember having a pretty strong sense of my self-worth and value even back then. It likely came from feeling well loved, well treasured, and well protected, like how a rare find or beloved artifact would have been. That was me. I was the beloved artifact, the remnant from a time in my mom's life that she was particularly fond of, a human vestige of sorts. As a result, I always felt very loved and treasured.

Thinking about my childhood home, that three-bedroom, one-bath brick ranch on Sargent's Drive, is not difficult. I remember there was a carport instead of a garage at the back of the house, where the main entrance was. Nobody used the front door, nobody we knew. The front entrance, with its welcoming portico, was reserved for the postman, door-to-door salesmen, and the occasional Jehovah's Witness. The back door off the carport was where the people we knew knocked while turning the doorknob to come in. That door opened into a small eat-in kitchen, which was the heart of our home. I remember it was wrapped with that fake wood paneling that they must have been giving away during the late '60s and early 70s. I remember every house from back then was covered wall-to-wall and room to room with vinyl paneling masquerading as wood. The kitchen table and chairs where we ate all our meals were made of solid wood and had a western theme. Six vintage spoked high-backed chairs with rustic design etchings sat around an oval table made of solid wood. The flooring throughout the house consisted of a geometric patterned linoleum in the kitchen and various carpet colors and textures throughout the rest of the house. Olive green carpet in the living room, red shag carpet in some of the bedrooms, "carpet sets" that included rugs and toilet tank covers in the bathroom, and other miscellaneous square and oval throw rugs concluded the list of non-matching tapestries. Today, I would describe the look as "vintage grandma," but trust me, back then, it was all in style and in line with the times.

I remember home being a comfortable and cozy place. We had heat and central air, indoor plumbing, a built-in washer and dryer, and a refrigerator freezer combination with a separate stand-alone freezer in the utility room adjacent to the carport filled with sustenance. My brother and I had our own bedrooms, as did Mom. We all shared one bathroom in the home, and it never seemed like that big of a deal. By society's standards, we were doing okay, and frankly, we were doing a lot better than some of the kids I knew. Today, after visiting and even owning homes two, three, and sometimes four times its size, I have come to realize that my childhood home was not just *cozy* in feeling. It was also very *cozy* in size. Meaning it was small - a lot smaller than I thought it was when I was little. We had some elbow room, but not a lot. Although our fake-wood paneled brick ranch with its kaleidoscope carpets lacked a highly coveted second bathroom, an extra bedroom for guests, or a formal dining room for holidays and special occasions, it still possessed everything I needed to thrive. I know this because not only did I thrive back then, but I am still thriving. In contrast, I can tell you stories of people I know who, despite growing up in mansions (compared to my childhood home), did not, and in many ways, are still not thriving.

Did you know most people end up spending up to 75% of their time in the same rooms of any home? This is despite the total number of rooms a house may have, with the top spots being the master bedroom – 6.8 hours per day; the living room – 4.4 hours per day; the office/study – 3.3 hours per day; and the kitchen/dining room – 2.1 hours per day. (**Darbyshire, W. (2020, December 21). The Best Value for Money. https://movinghomeadvice.com/featured/revealed-which-room-of-the-house-gives-the-best-value-for-money/.**) Our movements in the spaces that make up our home follow a familiar pattern, usually one

> I remember home being a comfortable and cozy place.

carried over from childhood into adulthood. As a result, my favorite spaces in any place I call home are: (1) the family room, (2) the kitchen, (3) the bedroom, and (4) the patio, lanai, or outdoor space, if applicable. For me, the family room (or casual living room) is the most important room in the house, both when I was a kid and now. Back then, it was the place where we sat, played games, snuggled, watched TV, looked through photo albums, browsed retail catalogs from Sears, JC Penny, or Service Merchandise, opened Christmas presents, munched on snacks, and so on. The same holds true in my home today, except for browsing old retail catalogs or photo albums. Instead, you will find us using a phone, laptop, or iPad to browse the stores of any number of retailers online. As for old photos, instead of photo albums, pictures are constantly looping through a digital picture frame that sits on the same stand as our HD TV.

The kitchen is my next favorite spot because that is where all the best smells come from. My mom made home-cooked meals every day for almost every meal. Breakfast was one of my favorites. I was never really a morning person growing up, but the smell of bacon was a sure bet at getting me up and moving. Fried fish on Fridays or fried chicken on Sundays, made with love in that tiny kitchen, make up warm and treasured memories for me. Next is the bedroom, which was and will always be my sanctuary. It was my safe and quiet place to retreat to when things got too hectic at home. The bedroom was where I read, played music, wrote in my journal, and made sense of the world. It has always been the place where I could rest peacefully and recharge my batteries.

Last on my list is the outdoor space. Ironically, my childhood home did not have a porch or patio area. Even though we had a large backyard, there was no designated place to sit, eat meals, or fellowship with friends and family outdoors. I am not even sure whether that was a "thing" back then, but I remember attending some outdoor parties as a kid and thinking about how nice it was, in the spring and fall, that is. I have always enjoyed being outdoors, under blue or star-filled skies. Today, especially since the COVID pandemic, it is one of my favorite places to enjoy quality time with friends and family. It gave the phrase "*we outside*" new meaning. Many people agree with the adage, "*The kitchen is the heart of the home.*" For others, the bathroom is the ultimate sanctuary. The most important room could be a bedroom, a den, or even a game room. There are no rules set in stone regarding this. The most important room in the house will vary from person to person. The fact remains that wherever we call home, we tend to confine ourselves to the same few rooms or spaces, and these spaces give us the most comfort, security, and joy.

- 2 -

Reflections in the Review

My earliest recollection of home includes the story of my parents, who became homeowners before I was born. In the late `60s, my dad, a career U.S. Marine, met my mom, a divorced homemaker and single mother. Their meeting lit a fire that cleared the way for my very existence. They were married a brief time later. Before my conception, my parents and my four-year-old brother started their journey together as a family of three. They ended up living in what I call a "starter home." Ironically, it was the same house my mom and her first husband (my brother's father) started in but never finished in. Of course, back then, this notion of a "starter home" was not exactly popular, if it existed at all. If you were fortunate enough to build or buy a house of your own, you typically started and ended right there in that same house. My parents' house was in an up-and-coming neighborhood a few miles from the Paris Island Marine Corps Recruit Training base in South Carolina. This house was also less than twenty miles from where my mom was born and raised.

My dad was a career Marine, meaning he could have been deployed anywhere in the world. As life would have it, they ended up only a few miles from Mom's birthplace. Their house and community were already filled with memories and history long before my mom and dad attempted to make new history of their own. Mom was born on one of the Gullah or Geechie islands of South Carolina in the "Lowcountry." This region consists of barrier islands in the US southeast along the coasts of North Carolina, South Carolina, and Georgia. It is home to a large population of the descendants of formerly enslaved West Africans who managed to retain most of the cultural heritage from their original homeland (countries like Senegal, Nigeria, Cameroon, and Sierra Leone).

As a result, early home life for my mom and others in her community contained the foods, music, language, agriculture, arts, crafts, and religious practices that sailed over with our ancestors on ships bound for what was called the "new world." Unlike the stories we learned in grade school about ships like the *Nina*, the *Pinta,* and the *Santa Maria*, I later learned about other ships that were just as pivotal to our nation's rich and complicated history. I remember when I first heard stories about the Mid-Atlantic slave trade. I thought it was right out of a horror movie! However, despite the atrocities that ensued, the richness and beauty of African culture managed to survive and endure through to today. In communities like those of the Gullah or Geechie people, certain words and phrases were passed down through multiple generations from languages spoken in the villages and tribes of their ancestral origins. My mom and the people in those Gullah communities grew up eating foods that many never knew where the original recipes came from, such as *jollof rice* (African), which is the same as *low country red rice* (Gullah).

Mom's journey is like many others from her day. She left the Deep South right after high school and hopped on a train headed north to stay with relatives in New York City, hoping to achieve more than the "Jim Crow" South could offer her. However, her experiences there taught her that the "more" that everyone was chasing did not compare to what she had left back home on those Gullah islands. She returned a short time later. Not long afterward, her journey continued. It included marriage, giving birth to a son, divorce, and a second marriage. The emotional and psychological distance between those two marriages was a far country. My Mom, her son, and her second husband made their home a house built and settled by working class African American military veterans. The street was aptly named "Sargent's Drive." Every home on this street was built and or occupied by men who had reached the rank of "Sargent," which is the highest rank for "non-commissioned" officers in the US armed services. Back then, Sargent was the ceiling for most Black military leaders.

My US Marine Corps 1st Sargent dad would be in good company with his Gunnery Sargent, Master Sargent, and Staff Sargent neighbors. They were modest homes built on one-quarter, one-third to one-half acre lots less than ten minutes from the front gates of the base. Unfortunately, their three-bedroom, one-bath brick ranch on Sargent's Drive was the place where this young family was forced to reckon with the news of my dad's stage IV lung cancer diagnosis. This news came around the same time that they learned about Mom's pregnancy with me. Back then, cancer treatments were not at all what they are today. The "Big C," was usually a death sentence. And it was for my dad. He lost a brief battle with the unrelenting and unsympathetic disease.

Lung cancer snatched my father from my mother's arms months after his initial diagnosis and exactly two weeks to the day before I was born. The honorable 1st Sargent was survived by his widow, a soon-to-be six-year-old boy (my brother), and the unborn me. My mom was forced to find the strength to figure out how to make that three-bedroom, one-bath brick ranch feel like home in the aftermath of the unexpected loss of her second husband. Despite unbearable grief, the trauma of childbirth, and the stress of managing life as a newly widowed parent of two, that modest three-bedroom one-bath brick ranch on Sargent's Drive became the first home I ever knew. I was the infant brought home from the hospital by that grieving wife and mother. I now know that through that experience, through that lens, I learned how important the sense of "home" is to one's overall well-being, my mom's, my brother's, and my own. Perhaps that is why the West Africans who were snatched from their homeland and forced to settle on those sea islands hundreds of years ago held so tightly to those things and customs that reminded them of home. Perhaps that sense of home helped them through their agonizing trauma and grief as well.

As I ponder my early memories of home, I cannot help but think about my husband's recollections and how different his are from mine. Early on in our relationship, he shared stories, lots of them, about his humble beginnings. For example, he joked about not having much in the way of a bedroom growing up. It was described as a literal closet with a twin-sized bed. He grew up poor and knew it. He was not like some people I know who boast about growing up poor but not knowing it because everyone else around them was living in the same circumstances. That is a whole different kind of poverty, one that does not call attention to your lack or highlight how insignificant or forgotten you feel. His reality was he did not have a bedroom closet. His bedroom was the closet and there was not much to put in it. This is undoubtedly why our bedroom is such an important room to him in our house. The size of the room, especially the closet space, is essential to him.

> Perhaps that sense of home helped them through their agonizing trauma and grief as well.

Fortunately, the favor of God was working on his behalf, and he was blessed down through the years. He transitioned out of poverty long before we met and now enjoys the lifestyle and possessions, he only dreamed about having when he was a kid. During the extent of our marriage alone, my husband's collection of clothes, shoes, neckties, and jewelry has grown exponentially. So yes, closet space and design are a huge deal for us! Also, as important, if not more important than the bedroom closet for my husband is the kitchen. He loves to cook. Cooking would be his love language if Gary Chapman added it to his famous list of *Five*. He has been cooking for himself and his family since he was a little boy. Cooking and eating together brought a sense of comfort and security during difficult times.

The process for figuring out what our dream relationship should look like is the same as what I suggested we do before purchasing our dream house. We must look back in that rearview mirror to our childhood for clues. This may be particularly challenging for those raised in a single-parent home. I recall my experience growing up in a one-parent home. Although my dad was deceased and my mom was raising my brother and me alone, I felt completely loved every day. I did not feel his absence caused me to suffer from any lack of parental love. It was probably because something happens to widowed parents of young children. I think parenting styles change after the unexpected loss of the other parent. The surviving parent either withdraws from the child or children, OR they cling to them very tightly. Withdrawal usually results from the pain of grief and loss intensifying when that child or children are nearby. Seeing your lost loved one through the eyes and other features of their kids can be too much for some parents to bear. Children are walking and talking reproductions of their parents, and that reality can be difficult for the surviving parent to face every day.

On the other hand, the love that the surviving parent has for their kids can feel stronger and more intense, especially immediately following the other parent's passing. I believe that comes from the need to find a place for all that displaced love and affection, assuming there was love and affection to begin with. The grieving parent may compensate for their loss by filling up the recently vacated spaces in their heart with their kids. My mom did the latter, perhaps because the love she shared with her husband was still new at the time of his passing. There was no baggage, no bad memories, or years where their love had grown cold or stale. All the love they shared, their hopes, dreams, and adoration for each other had a short lifespan. The magnitude of their love seemed to transfer to me the moment my dad took his last breath.

After my dad's death, I think my mother loved my brother and me more desperately than she would have otherwise. Because she never remarried, she never found another suitable object to pour some of that emotional energy into. It is said that "Too much of a good thing is not always such a good thing." That was certainly my story. I say that because over time, the weight of all my mom's displaced love and affection and the expectations that came with it sometimes felt too heavy for me to bear. Do not get me wrong, it is always good to be loved and know you are loved, but not all love feels good. That is less of a complaint and more of an observation, but sometimes I felt that mom's love for her kids seemed a bit out of balance. In hindsight, I think I figured out at an early age that my only recourse was to gain my independence as soon as possible. I remember thinking that Mom's love sounded "needy" and felt desperate. I was learning just how desperately she needed us to need her. I later learned the term for the "needy pattern" I was trying to avoid. It is called *codependency*. There was no frame of reference for it when I was a kid, but somehow, I instinctively knew it was not good. It is kind of funny when I think about it now. Family members who remember me as a toddler all remark at how impressed they were with my independence at an early age. I was walking at nine months old, getting my own food and anything else I wanted by age two, and not wanting much help unless it was absolutely necessary. Hindsight has also helped me see how this shaped my relationship patterns.

I first thought that finding someone who was as woefully independent as I was, meaning someone with no chance of being too dependent or codependent, was the way to go. Then, in my mind, at least, I felt their love could not drown me. Before I met my husband,

> The magnitude of their love seemed to transfer to me the moment my dad took his last breath.

one serious relationship that almost resulted in marriage was with someone exactly like that. We were good friends who greatly admired each other and fell deeply in love. His personality is one that I would describe as *stoic,* meaning he had a very calm and super self-controlled demeanor. I looked it up to make sure my label for him was fitting, and I found that the Oxford Pocket Dictionary of Current English defines a stoic as "a person who can endure pain or hardship without showing their feelings or complaining." Don't get me wrong, he was kind and very supportive of me, but this was the exact opposite of the type of love I had known as a kid. He was exactly what I thought I wanted, but not at all what I ultimately needed. I never felt "at home" in that relationship. I later realized that I needed a healthier and more balanced version of the type of love I experienced as a kid.

I strongly believe, and studies have shown that whether we like it or not, our parents shape how we give and receive love. Have you ever noticed how people end up marrying someone who resembles their mom or dad, in terms of personality that is? The same principle is held even when you have not been raised by your biological parents. The people who raise and nurture you as a child leave a permanent impression on you. Despite feeling a little smothered and troubled by her lack of boundaries, I felt the most loved and at home with my mom. The relationship between parents and kids can be complicated, but what is never complicated is the security that comes from feeling loved by them. Feeling secure and loved by your parent or parents is the driving force behind every committed relationship.

> Our parents shape how we give and receive love.

We either long for what we had and did not think we needed or long for what we needed and did not feel that we had as children. In my marriage, I ended up with a version of what I had as a kid but did not think I needed. My husband's story is the exact opposite of mine. He would say that he ended up with what he needed but never thought he had as a child. In his case, neither parent imparted a strong sense of fondness or security, but the same driving forces held true. If you did not feel unconditionally loved or secure as a child, you will most certainly long for it as an adult. The caution, however, is to be careful about seeking familiarity with what "home" was like growing up. If home for you as a child was a toxic and unhealthy environment, then you may seek it out or settle for it without fully understanding why. This is why we must carefully consider and evaluate what "home" looked like for us as kids, being honest about what was good and what was not.

Big Reveal #1

For clues on which direction to take in pursuing your dream house or dream relationship, it is important to consider your past experiences to better understand what will likely work best for you moving forward.

Helpful Scriptures

"This is what the Lord Almighty says:
'Give careful thought to your ways',"
Haggai 1:7 (NIV)

"I remember the days of long ago; I meditate on all Your works and consider what Your hands have done,"
Psalms 143:5 (NIV)

- 3 -

Focus on the "Must Haves"

This isn't limited to Barbie. Whether you're living at home, sharing a space, or owning, you've likely daydreamed about your ideal home. Occasionally, though, I encounter people who say they're content with renting and have no desire to buy a home. They reason that renting eliminates the need for maintenance and long-term commitments. While that could be accurate, I think most individuals can be categorized into either of two groups: those who own homes and those who aspire to do so. Sometimes, those who fall under the first category are not completely satisfied and find themselves still in pursuit of their "ideal" or "dream home." That means they are contemplating whether to renovate and remodel the home they have or whether to trade up for something new. The second category, the "aspiring" bunch, describes folks who have never committed to purchasing a home. Sometimes it is because home ownership requires just that, a "commitment."

A thirty-year or even a fifteen-year mortgage differs greatly from the one year or month-to-month lease agreements that often come with renting. There are several reasons people end up in this category, besides the obvious one: *commitment issues.* Considering what is required for home ownership these days, it simply boils down to not being willing to, not being able to, or a combination of the two. I believe that everyone — buyers and renters alike will at some point ponder all their home ownership possibilities. It is this contemplation that motivates and inspires a person to take the required steps toward home ownership. Unfortunately, fear, self-doubt, and negative thoughts can drown out those dreams, causing people to settle for their current living arrangements. They ultimately cannot find the courage to level up to something greater.

Dreaming about home ownership and taking steps to achieve home ownership are two different things altogether. Once you decide to commit, one of the most important first steps are figuring out what you would *like to have* in your new home versus the things you feel you must *have.* Determining what you can actually afford comes next. I believe that making a list of *must haves* should come first, even before setting the budget. This may go against what you have been taught or your own practical wisdom. The reason I say make the *must have* list first is because if you go after this major purchase with only budget in mind, you may never end up with what your heart truly desires or anything close to it. Your purchase should reflect your personality and even your purpose.

First, figure out your *must haves*, those things that create a sense of comfort for you, or delight your senses, or give you a sense of security. Only then should you determine your budget. Your budget simply quantifies how much you can spend on your *must haves list.* This list of things, sometimes tangible and sometimes not, is unique to every individual. During the house hunting process, a realtor will ask a series of questions to help the potential buyer identify what those "must haves" are. These questions help reveal what the chief

> Your purchase should reflect your personality and even your purpose.

priorities are for the buyer. Home buyer priorities include things like location, style, size (square footage), layout, configuration, multi-level vs single-story, number of bedrooms, number of bathrooms, and other amenities such as swimming pools, hot tubs, or even outdoor kitchens. Of course, the home buyer's budget will always test the true limits of their priorities. The amount of money the buyer is qualified to spend coupled with their ideal preferences will certainly help to narrow down the many purchase options.

Ideally, a realtor can lead the buyer to their dream home by getting to know the buyer more personally and weighing their must haves against their budget. Well beyond the purchase and move in date, a buyer's list of priorities (must haves) will continue to play a role in their overall satisfaction with their home. Sometimes, a reevaluation of those priorities can drive homeowners to consider taking on remodeling projects. Overhauling an outdated kitchen or extending a main bedroom and making it into a main suite are decisions based on what is most important to the homeowner. If the home buyer is anything like my husband with his passion for cooking and entertaining, buying a home with a gourmet kitchen or completely remodeling an existing one would be very high on his list of "must haves" for his "dream home". We agree with this priority, as we both enjoy cooking and entertaining. However, if we did not agree, our conflict, if coupled with a lack of compromise, would likely result in delays or missing out on our dream home altogether.

It is important to distinguish between the "dream home," the "starter home," and a "rental home." Both the rental and the starter home help meet our housing needs for safe shelter. Unfortunately, sometimes in our zeal to show the world and ourselves that we have "arrived," we cannot see and fully appreciate the blessings found in what we have right now. Sure, it is good to have grand goals and aspirations, but some of life's best joys can only be found along the way while we are moving on up like *George and Weesie* on the classic 70s sitcom *The Jeffersons*.

With your *must haves* list in hand, you can move forward with your home buying or remodeling plans. There are some specific areas in which you need to know whether you're willing to compromise. This first area of consideration is location. In the world of real estate, it is said that the three most important factors are "location, location, and location".

- 4 -

Focus on the "Must Haves"

This seems like the perfect time to highlight one of those marriage parallels I mentioned earlier. Just like with the "dream house," we all have our own vision of what our ultimate partnership or "dream marriage" looks like, or at least we should before we make that commitment. Whether you are single (never married), currently married, or divorced; you probably have thought a lot about relationships and what your dream partner and partnership should look like. Hopefully, you have also figured out whether you have a "buying" versus a "renting" mindset. If you truly are a "buyer" and not a perpetual "renter," there are a few things you may want to consider before making plans for marriage.

Think about the *must have* list, only for your relationships instead of real estate. Do you want a marriage that is more traditional in terms of roles and responsibilities, or one that is more modern? Do you prefer your relationship to be closed off from others (compartmentalized) or do you prefer more of an open concept, having plenty of space to include relationships with extended family and friends? Are you seeing the similarities? The very steps I suggested taking before deciding on a new home are like the steps you should take before choosing a spouse or life partner.

Remember that little exercise of reflecting on those childhood memories for insights into what you would want in your new home? Well, that exercise is even more helpful in determining what will and will probably NOT work for you in your marriage. The word *"reflection"* describes the act of looking forward to an image that is in front of you from the perspective of looking back, as with a mirror. While you are looking forward to the image of who you think you are, you are at the same time looking back at yourself through the lens of who you actually are, which is based on who you have been in the past. Let's back up a bit because as I am writing this, I can see how what I just said may sound a little confusing, so let me rephrase it. More simply put, during the process of reflection, your current likes and dislikes coexist with your past preferences and patterns. Therefore, it is so important to understand how your past experiences have shaped your current day's likes and dislikes.

Prior to marriage, or any serious committed partnership, it is important to take time for self-evaluation so you can identify what your relationship priorities are and what your list of desired qualities is in a mate. More importantly, we must determine how compatible those desires, preferences and "must haves" are with your potential mate and their priorities. For people of faith, an added step is to make sure that your priorities are not only compatible with your mate but are also compatible with your faith. This additional step is more than a "make a list" or "create a vision board" type of exercise. It involves hours of prayer, meditation, and the counsel from trusted clergy or other trusted spiritual leaders. Again, the process is intentional, personal, and unique to the individual. With that said, I believe we are each designed with a unique set of traits (skills and natural abilities) and personal preferences.

> Identify what your relationship priorities are and what your list of desired qualities is in a mate.

For example, people have described me as intuitive, kind, thoughtful, friendly, calm under pressure, analytical, and someone with excellent communication, people, and leadership skills. Although I am certain that a lot of other people possess those same traits, the exact combination of my traits is unique to me. The same holds true for my personal preferences. I enjoy being creative. Writing is the medium that I get the most enjoyment from, which I feel aligns perfectly with my sense of purpose. Also on my creative side is my love of music. I enjoy listening to music of all kinds. I even took piano lessons as a kid, but it never sparked the selfish devotion you need to be a talented musician. Instead I resigned myself to becoming an aficionado, or ultimate fan. I am the one who appreciates and consumes the art produced by others, admiring the fruits of their labor instead of my own. I love nature, leisure travel, and exploring different cultures. These, coupled with my skills and natural abilities, make me one of a kind. That is why there is no cookie cutter model or design that appeals to everyone, not in real estate or relationships. I like what I like, and you like what you like. We may like some of the same things, but never to the same degree.

Before I met my husband, I was still on the road figuring out what my desires and preferences were in a mate. He and I laugh to this day about an informal list that I carried in the back of my mind about the type of man that I did *not* want to end up with. In hindsight, my list should have concentrated more on the qualities of the person who I wanted instead of the opposite. It was after we met and started dating that I realized the irony of my ridiculous "what I don't want" list. For example, I emphatically stated that I did not want to date preachers, pastors, or clergy of any kind. My rationale was simple. According to my worldview, the devout ones were already married to the church and who could compete with that. The ones in this category that were not as serious about their call to ministry were (according to me) usually whoring around boldly, or covertly under the watchful eyes of their congregants. I certainly had no desire to be under the scrutiny of those *watchful eyes.*

Another item on my "what I don't want list" was more superficial and had to do with physical appearances. I had a thing about a person's smile and their teeth. So basically, I had no interest in anyone who had gold or other precious metals replacing their original teeth. Unfortunately, I had adopted some negative stereotypes about people who opted for gold or silver caps or crowns. It is so funny because today, having a custom "grill" made of gold or silver embedded with diamonds is the ultimate fashion accessory, at least in certain sections of popular culture. Here's a brief history: Throughout the 50s, 60s, and 70s, when a crown was needed to repair a damaged tooth, gold was the preferred choice of those who really wanted to shine, especially in Black and Hispanic communities. Let's be honest, gold crowns cost more, so in a sense they helped to define your social status, especially in lower income communities. Using precious metals in dental work was common in many countries in Africa, the West Indies (Caribbean), and Asia.

The history of the practice, however, dates all the way back to the earliest civilizations. Anthropologists have discovered that the ancient Etruscans (Italy) had gold teeth as early as 700 B.C. In the Mayan (Mexico) culture, people were found with jade filled teeth. Jade is a gemstone with spiritual significance that was once considered more valuable than gold. Despite the rich history of the practice, I grew up in an era when this practice had lost most, if not all, of its appeal in mainstream society. I was in the camp that believed the people who still wore gold in their mouths were doing so because they had nothing of value to say or to offer. I am ashamed of holding such negative stereotypes now. My personal experiences have taught me that those beliefs could not be further from the truth. It is just another example of how strongly society can influence our beliefs and behaviors.

Continuing this review of my "do not want" list, I was also leery of anyone divorced, particularly those divorced with children. So, the reason my husband and I continue to laugh at my list throughout our years together is because he scored a perfect three out of three on what

I've listed so far. He was a Baptist preacher (1), he had a gold crown in the front of his smile with his initials engraved in it (2) and he was newly divorced with kids when we married with the youngest being his sixteen-year-old son. Note too self: Be careful about saying what you won't do. Despite this, what he had going for him was almost all the other qualities I knew I wanted and considered *must haves* for a life partner. I find it both funny and strange that I spent so much energy on what I wasn't looking for instead of placing the focus on what I valued and wanted most. I have since learned that I was not alone in my thinking.

A lot of other women have shared with me this negative approach to dating. Negative, as in focusing on the "NOT". How can you expect a positive outcome when your criteria are based on things that are negative? I believe that what you get is very much aligned with what you spend your focus on the most and what you most expect. Fostering negative perceptions about certain groups of people will almost always yield negative results because, for the most part, you will eventually either get what you expect or miss out completely on what you need the most. Instead, we should find out what qualities are most important to us and then look expectantly for them.

Fortunately for me, just prior to my husband and I getting together, I had already concluded that my way of looking at things and people needed a complete overhaul. I had already chucked that "do not want" list and made a new mental list of my must haves in a mate. If I had not discarded my previous list and changed my thinking, I may have missed out on the greatest love of my life. Here's what I realized I needed in my new *must have* list:

> I had already concluded that my way of looking at things and people needed a complete overhaul.

1   A man of faith, with a healthy fear of God. One of my favorite scriptures' states, "The fear of God is the beginning of wisdom." Let's be honest, nobody wants to play the fool or get stuck with one!

2   I wanted to be with someone with strong family ties and connections.

3   I needed to be with someone with a joyful heart, able to laugh with me through good and bad times to offer some balance to my super-serious side. Other qualities included a strong work ethic, solid or stable financial history (no bankruptcies), a stable work history, and someone friendly and comfortable in most, if not all, social settings. I considered these my *must have* essentials.

Based on past relationships, I additionally require a partner who can effectively communicate their feelings. Sure, I know the communication of feelings thing is a tall order for most people these days (especially men), but I remained hopeful that I would run across at least one I could work with. Another thing I figured out during many hours of self-reflection was that I express my love through the context of friendship. Therefore, I wanted to be with someone who understood and shared my friendship and partnership values. I wanted my life partner to have the same qualities that I would seek in a best friend.

The last thing I will mention was never really a *must have,* or at least I didn't think it was. It was something I never knew I needed until some years after I was married. A little fact about me: I love the beach! In fact, I love being near most bodies of water. It is near those places that I feel most at peace. Finding someone who could enjoy being at the beach or near water with me, as often as the mood strikes me, would be icing on the cake.

Getting to the point of knowing your personal "must haves" is significant, but there is also a list of basic needs that everyone shares. I feel it is only *after* the basic human or core needs are met that we can then look beyond them to reach our ultimate dreams and desires. My "must haves" list is void if my basic or core needs have not already been satisfied. All of humanity has a list of core needs that we all share. Most philosophers and psychologists agree and have explored this "core needs" concept in great detail.

For context, I will take some time to describe what a psychologist named Abraham Maslow wrote in his 1943 work entitled *A Theory of Human Motivation*. This paper was our first introduction to his now famous "Hierarchy of Needs" theory. A simple explanation of this theory is that there are specific levels of needs that all humans have in common and the things that motivate and drive us are attached to each of these levels. Since he's describing a hierarchy, the best graphical representation or picture of this would look like a triangle or pyramid with the most basic needs at the bottom and the higher, more complex needs at the top. Let's examine Maslow's triangle as a guide for examining compatibility with

> My "must haves" list is void if my basic or core needs have not already been satisfied.

a potential mate. The most basic level of needs (the bottom of the triangle) are our "Physiological" needs. These are the physical "must haves" for human survival. Things like clean air, water, food, sleep, clothing, shelter and, for adults, sex drive or sexual instinct. Before we go to the next level, let me clarify I am not suggesting that we must have all of our sexual needs and desires met before closing in on a potential mate. Not at all. However, having sexual interest or desire for your potential mate is very much a critical part of predicting whether your partner will help satisfy that basic human need for sex.

Once the physical needs are met, the next level up on the triangle are "Safety and Security" needs. Safety "must haves" include things like personal security, financial security, access to healthcare, and general wellbeing. For this level, when looking at a potential mate, consider things like current drug and alcohol use, mental health, history of unemployment, and any signs of physical, emotional, or even psychological aggressive behavior. Next are the "Love and Belonging" needs, which include relationships with others, communication with others, support systems, being part of a community, and feeling loved by others. For this level, look closely at how love is expressed toward you and others, look at each other's "tribe" or circle of friends and acquaintances, and most importantly pay close attention to current relationships with parents, siblings, or other members of a person's family of origin. Take the time to investigate and understand how these things may affect you in the future.

Next are what's known as the "Self-Esteem" needs. These are things like hope, joy, curiosity, happiness, and accepting oneself. We all have varying degrees of "self-esteem." What's critical here is determining which of these is lacking. A person with no hope or joy in their lives, or who hasn't learned to love themselves, is probably not in the best position to enter a long-term committed partnership like marriage. Last is referred to as "Self-Actualization" or "Self-Acceptance" needs, which are the highest level on Maslow's triangle. These needs are more intellectual and spiritual. They include things like thinking, learning, decision making, values, spiritual beliefs, fulfillment, and helping others.

Keep in mind that these levels are not suggestions, Maslow and others describe them as being essential needs for all human beings. For people of faith, the good news is that God has already promised to supply *all* our needs, which includes every level of that triangle. Inviting God to help fulfill his "need-supplying" promise will ready you for that dream house and dream relationship. So, if you are still struggling with the needs on the lower end of the triangle, such as physical and safety, you're probably not fully prepared to take on the type of project we're talking about in this book. That goes for a dream house as well as a dream relationship. The needs higher on the triangle are achieved over time and can sometimes be more quickly realized within healthy, committed relationships. The relationship does not meet the need, however, it hopefully provides a safe place for development. So, if our "belonging" or "self-actualization" (acceptance) needs have not been realized, a house or a relationship won't fix it. Your dream home or dream marriage is a by-product of having your core human needs satisfied. Again, the people of faith will hopefully remember that it is God who supplies all our needs, and we must constantly survey our lives for the evidence of this fundamental promise.

The important thing to remember in all of this is that it is only *after* our core needs are met (Physical, Safety/Security, Love and Belonging) that we can truly grow and prosper. Also, it is *while* we grow that we can see our progress and can visualize ourselves bigger, better, or greater than before. It is in our desire for greater that we dream bigger dreams. We begin to long for those qualities, features, people, and things that meet or exceed our expectations. All this growth, progress, and satisfaction with higher needs (Self- Esteem and Self-Actualization) result in more extraordinary results and perhaps a different *must have* list than you started out with. Our *must have* list can look different from what it did during our earlier stages. Wait, am I suggesting that the "must have" list that I initially create for myself is going to change over time? It may and probably will. This is because the things we value the most often change at different stages of our lives.

> It is in our desire for greater that we dream bigger dreams.

However, when it comes to marriage, it is extremely important that both parties share the same or similar values before they decide to make the commitment. One common misconception is that "shared values" equate to "shared or similar personalities". That does not always hold true. Prime example, my husband has a loud, very outgoing personality and is known as the "comedian" within our circle of friends. I, too, am fairly outgoing but have a more reserved way of interacting with people. When we first got together, he was drawn to reality-based shows, TV judge shows, what I call Paternity TV, and other melodramas. I am a self-described, quintessential geek, preferring nature and science-based shows, documentaries about interesting people or events, travel and home improvement shows, and a few dramatic series sprinkled in now and again but only if they are very well written. Our entertainment tastes were as different as popcorn and pizza, but our lists of "must-haves" within the context of our relationship were very similar.

For example, having the same or similar faith, or religious beliefs, is extremely important to us both, but it goes way beyond that. When you peel the layers back and look at the role our faith plays in our everyday lives, especially the decisions we make, you see that my husband and I are almost identical. We are "cut from the same cloth" as the old saying goes. The spiritual foundation that formed us, both as individuals and later as a couple, was made from similar material. Because of that foundation, we were able to quickly determine that our spiritual paths aligned. When we realized we were heading in the same direction, we had to agree on the best way to get there. That is a more difficult achievement. Two adults of the opposite sex rarely agree on the best way to get anywhere.

Women like to read maps and plan, all while having packed and prepared for the worst-case scenario. Men, on the other hand, know the way, even when they don't, and can sometimes be reluctant to admit the obvious and ask for much needed directions. While preparing for marriage and even early in our marriage, my husband and I checked in with each other and compared notes on what our next moves should be, particularly who would do what. Although he jokingly says that I am the one who makes the decisions and he follows, that was never and is not at all the case. He has always been very visionary in terms of where he sees us in the future. He is a dreamer at heart. It is true that I am the "Let's stay in the moment" person in our relationship, but I am sometimes guilty of analyzing those moments a little too much. On a bad day, I may fall into the trap of comparing the here and now with our hopeful future plans, or other past times in our lives, or worse yet, other people.

Be forewarned, comparing your "right now" to anything or anyone else is a very slippery slope! Deciding on the best way of getting anywhere is a lot like rowing. You can throw two people in a boat with some oars and point them to an island of paradise with the goal of getting there, but if those two don't communicate and agree on the process, they are in for a stressful and exhausting journey if they make it there at all. My husband and I figured out our rhythm fairly early in our marriage. I think prayer was and still is key to our success. We are at our best when we follow this pattern: (1) We share our dreams, vision, and desires for the future with each other, (2) pray (separately and together) about those plans asking God for direction and provision. (3) share with each other what we think we heard God say. (4) Agree on the next steps. (5) move or row forward in faith.

After agreeing on where we're headed, we next had to figure out if we were traveling at the same pace. Would we be walking in lockstep with each other, or would one of us leave the other behind? I have come to realize that determining our pace and rhythm could only be revealed through a spiritual evaluation. I say spiritual because for me, the question whether you and your partner are knitted together enough to move forward together at a proper pace has very little to do with finances, childhood backgrounds, social status, education, etc. I remember being faced with the decision of whether my husband was the one God sent for me. After he made his intentions clear, I had to decide for myself whether to take that leap of faith. I did this by first asking myself two questions. (1) Do we both have a personal relationship with God? (2) Are we at the same or similar level of maturity, both spiritually and otherwise? The answer was yes to both, so I permitted myself to go deeper in my evaluation of him and our potential future together. If the answer to either of these questions is "no", then you are likely not adequately equipped or ready to enter the lifelong commitment of marriage. If one person has a personal relationship with God and the other does not, then a marriage or serious relationship will never reach its fullest potential for long-lasting joy, love, and fulfillment because there is an inherent conflict at the start that must be resolved in order for God's perfect plan for marriage to be fulfilled. If you both have a personal relationship with God, then the next question is almost as important as the first, and it is simply, how mature is your relationship with God?

Spiritual compatibility and maturity are key concepts that absolutely must be explored before you commit yourself to another. This can be looked at in the same way that we look at developmental maturity (physical age). Predictions of compatibility and sustainability for any serious committed relationship are based on whether the persons are operating at the same or similar levels of maturity. If one person has matured and developed well into their 50s and 60s and their mate is a late teen/young adult, I would venture to say that any serious partnership likely will not work and will fail the test of time. Longevity and success are more likely when two people are at the same stage of social, emotional, and psychological development. Spiritual compatibility works the same way. It's about your "stage" and not your "age". Because of this, it is possible for a person who has been in the church their whole lives to have the same or similar level of spiritual maturity as a new convert. There is so much we can explore on this topic, but I feel the need to bring us back to our main focus.

To recap, the process I have described so far includes identifying your "must haves", determining to what degree your core needs have been met and establishing whether the person or thing you are excited about right now is really the right one for the long haul. This sequence applies to both real estate and relationships. These are the building blocks for your "dream home" and your "dream relationship." If you have completed the steps I've described so far, you are well on your way to finding long-lasting joy and contentment. But wait a minute. You may be asking yourself, "What if I have already made my choice and committed to something or someone without doing the work you just suggested beforehand?" No worries. It is never too late, but it may require quite a lot more work after the fact. The process remains the same. Although these steps are meant to be proactive, you can always adjust and make them reactive. If you don't know what your priorities and preferences are, take some time and figure them out. If your core needs have not been met, work toward achieving them. If you don't know how compatible you are with your mate or have realized you aren't as compatible (having the same level of maturity), then work toward it, find common ground, nurture, and inspire growth and demand productivity. If your house doesn't meet your functional needs, remodel it. Your future happiness, joy, and success depends on it!

Big Reveal #2

Understand your own personal needs and values before committing to a major home purchase, renovation project, or relationship. Make sure that the venture is compatible with your values and vision for success.

Helpful scriptures

"Put your outdoor work in order and get your fields ready; after that, build your house."
Proverbs 24:27 (ESV)

"And God is able to bless you abundantly, so that in all things at all times, having all that you need, you will abound in every good work."
II Cor 9:8 (NIV)

"Can two people walk together without agreeing on the direction?"
Amos 3:3 (NLT)

- 5 -

Counting Up the Cost

"How much does it cost?" versus "How much I can afford?" is the dilemma facing all home buyers. When I was single and buying my first home, I remember filling out one of those online mortgage calculators. This special calculator is a tool that you can use prior to submitting a formal mortgage application that will tell you how much house you can afford based on the values you put in. Those tools are not detailed and rarely factor in your existing debt or expenses (your financial baggage), but you can plug in a sample home price, and it will calculate the mortgage principal, taxes, insurance, and the approximate down payment amount. I never would have submitted a formal loan application without first having run the numbers through the calculator tool.

Besides new home purchases, home renovation projects have become one of the more popular trends in the past fifteen years. In part because of the rise in home improvement based reality shows and the popularity of the hosts of those shows within our popular culture. More homeowners were fixing up their homes with the intention of either living in them much longer than expected or with the intention to "flip," which means to resell the home for a profit after renovations. French country kitchens with farmhouse sinks, modern quartz tops for counters or a waterfall edge on islands, shiplap and bead board accent walls, all became coveted must haves for homeowners in recent years. Contractors and interior designers are always eager to help homeowners achieve their dreams, but they will inevitably ask the same question, "What is your budget?"

Most people have had some experience with budgets. Budgeting is an accounting principle. It describes the planning and management of cash flow. Budgeting is a process that helps you save or set aside money so you can reach your financial goals. For some, budgeting is a very formal and rigid process of mapping total income to individual expected and unexpected expenses. For others, budgeting is more of an informal process of looking at how much total money you estimate having at the beginning of each month and figuring out how much you can spend before the money runs out. Despite it being associated with accounting (aka math) it is a simple concept. Budgeting is also an important first step to take before making any large purchases, such as buying a car, a home or taking on a major home renovation. There are certain types of projects that you cannot even start until you know what your budget is. Let's look at vacations as an example. When looking to book travel anywhere for any non-work-related, "pleasure based" reason, after deciding where you would like to go and for how long, your next ideal step is determining how much you will spend. This process involves looking up prices for things like lodging, travel, and entertainment (i.e. events tickets, tours or other excursions). Then food and beverage costs will need to be factored in for each day of your trip. In the end, we sometimes discover that our desires are far out of reach of our reality. Adjustments will have to be made to better align the two.

> Budgeting is an accounting principle.

Before purchasing our current home, my husband and I meticulously reviewed our finances to determine our affordability. This discussion included reviewing what it would take to pay the mortgage while maintaining a comfortable standard of living after the purchase. The purchase price is only part of the story. The mortgage consists of mandatory monthly payments that apply to the principal (or balance due) on the house based on the terms (length of mortgage plus interest rate). The monthly payment comprises the principal payment plus interest, as well as separate prorated amounts for things like property insurance, flood insurance and taxes. The bank pre-approved us for a certain amount based on the income and debts they could verify, but the bank is not all knowing. The bank did not know all there was to know about us. The bank didn't know about our spending, giving, or living habits. Once the bank gave us their numbers, we counted up the cost and came up with our own numbers that were based on our knowledge of our own personal budget. It was only after we knew what we could actually afford that we started any serious house hunting looking for properties that satisfied our "must have" criteria, but within a specific price range. Sometimes the "sticker shock" of what we think we must have caused us to reevaluate those stylish, trendy elements we deemed a necessity.

Location was our key priority when looking to buy our home, everything else lined up behind in order of importance. This order of priority is so important when considering what you can afford. I agree with most real estate professionals who affirm that location is the most important factor for home buying. You can add or remove features of a home, and even change its layout, but you can't change its location or the things that surround that location. What will the view outside your bedroom or living room window be overlooking? How far is the homesite from the things or the people you enjoy most? How would you describe the neighborhood and is it one that you would feel comfortable living in? These are just a few questions I would ask myself. For some, locations can be a source of compromise, for others, it is non-negotiable. Whichever way you prioritize location;

it is a key factor and a starting point for your home search. House hunting apps like Zillow, Trulia, Redfin or Realtor.com will help you refine your search results when you enter your desired location and filter by things like price range, home type, and home features (i.e. pool, views, etc.) The question we must all answer is how much house can I afford in my desired location?

- 6 -

Counting Up the Cost

Establishing a budget is necessary when embarking on any home buying or home remodeling journey, but what about marriage? It does not seem appropriate to set a "budget" for a relationship, as this term does not fit the definition. As I mentioned, budgeting deals with determining how much money is available to spend toward a specific venture or for overall lifestyle management. Money is a thing of value that has limited availability. It requires careful and purposeful management to ensure that we do not exhaust or over run its supply. If we substitute money for other things of value, then this same concept can apply to relationships as well. How is that? Because, practically speaking, budgeting is merely counting up the cost of what you want and then deciding how much you are willing or able to pay for it. We rarely have an unlimited budget for things that we desire. Most times, we are limited not only by the amount of money or other things of value that we possess, but also by certain fixed or predetermined costs we must pay along the way.

With relationships, what you *pay* is anything of value that you give to maintain a healthy and happy union. Sometimes there are things you may *pay for* in relationships, much like in home buying, that you consider negotiable while others are most certainly not. In accounting, money is the thing that we use to pay for what we want, and it is measured and managed accordingly. In relationships, what I pay or give in relationships are the things that I value most. This list includes things like my time, emotional support, financial support, spiritual support (i.e., prayers), energy, loyalty, friendship, and, of course, love. In our relationships, it is important to learn how to measure and manage these valuable resources as well. If not, we may exhaust or over run their supply. A certain level of maturity and awareness is needed to the point of knowing where the source of these resources comes from and, more importantly, how to replenish them so that you never run out. Time management, financial management, emotional intelligence, spirituality, and physical and emotional self-care are a few of the valuable resources that are needed for successful relationships.

Previous relationships serve as useful teachers for this relationship budgeting concept. My relationship budgeting skills were put to the test during my first serious relationships in young adulthood. At any stage, relationships will reflect our physical, emotional, and spiritual values and spending habits. There were times I felt that I had spent all I had on people whom I felt I shared a deep and meaning full connection with. I found that some of those relationships quickly depleted my resources, while others surprisingly nurtured and replenish them. The good news is that despite their outcome, all relationship experiences are profitable. Wisdom and lessons learned are gained with each one.

> Previous relationships serve as useful teachers for this relationship budgeting concept.

My lessons learned included how not to spend too many of my resources too soon in a relationship. I also learned how to quickly discern the degree to which a person could give me what I wanted and needed in the relationship. I learned about give and take and determined what my personal worth and value were. It did not take very many relationships to figure out whether the people I allowed access to me were worth the risk and the sacrifice. I eventually got pretty good at identifying the *givers* versus people just in it for the take. I do not know very many people who master relationship budgeting straight out of the gate. It usually takes some fine tuning, practice, discipline, and, for me, a lot of prayer.

Whether the topic is money or marriage, the budgeting process includes figuratively writing a much needed "reality check." So often our desires and expectations seem reasonable enough until we ask, "Can I afford this?" Affordability refers to determining whether you possess the required resources and capacity to get what you desire to purchase or gain. We commonly look at affordability in financial terms, but like budgeting, it can apply to both accounting and non-accounting principles. You may want to buy a new car, for example. Not just any new car, but that European luxury make and model you've been dreaming about. Before going to the dealership and talking to the salesman, you probably should figure out whether you have the down payment, the credit score, or the monthly income needed to purchase that car. Not only do you need to determine your financial ability to purchase your dream car, but you also must consider what it will take to maintain it. Can you afford it? Taking it a step further, if you are a person of faith, you must also take time to consider how what you desire fits within God's plans. Will getting what you desire be a help or a hindrance? Whether you identify as Christian, Jewish, Muslim, some other faith, or no faith at all, it is important to note this point: timing is everything.

As a Christian, I used to think that discerning God's plan, and not only His plan but His timing, was some kind of a mystical event that could only be revealed after completing a strenuous task or ritual like fasting or reading the Bible three times a day for a year. I have often struggled with the notion of purpose and divine plan. It was during those struggles that the secret was revealed. The best way to find out what God's plans are and how you can best serve His plans is to ask Him directly during prayer time and by reading and studying His written words. Yes, it is as simple as it sounds. For me, prayer is not a ritual. It is simply having a candid conversation with the Creator, or God. Those with no faith may struggle with this notion. An atheist, for example, would probably choose to have candid conversations with people they think are more knowledgeable or wise than they are. People of faith, however, all agree that the Creator is the only true source of wisdom. Frequent prayer (having candid conversations with God) and meditation (sitting quietly and focused as you wait to hear His voice) is extremely beneficial to understanding our worth, our value, our budget, and the cost of getting the things or the people we desire. Studying God's word is also beneficial. Which is probably why I was given a Bible immediately following my baptism. Although, since I was thirteen, I am sure it did not get as much use as was intended. At some point in time in my life, I finally got around to reading the famous book. In it, I found comforting promises, clear directions, careful warnings, and compassionate love letters. For me, the Bible has been the best, most helpful instruction manual I have received. Certainly, it has proven better than the one that came with my latest car, or the ones that come with those "assembly required" pieces of furniture. In each of those cases, the manuals fell short. They either failed to cover every problem, or they resulted in ending up with extra miscellaneous parts (like screws, nuts, or bolts) leaving you to question whether they were simply extras or critical parts in the overall product design.

> I found comforting promises, clear directions, careful warnings, and compassionate love letters.

However, God's instructions for humanity, found in sacred books, seem to cover it all. I believe that anything extra in them can prove useful as well. A scripture in the bible puts it this way, "All Scripture is God-breathed and is useful for teaching, rebuking, correcting and training," II Timothy 3:16 (NIV). This does not mean that the "words of God" that have been recorded on ancient scrolls and then written and rewritten throughout history in various sacred texts are not without flaws. Both theologians and historians agree to the evidence of some inconsistencies and cultural influences that have been "added" throughout the years. One of our inherit flaws as humans is to "ad lib" to what we hear or have been taught. We add our own interpretation, or our own "spin" to things. Even with this challenge, one can search the scriptures by topic or specific circumstances and find examples of life's problems and answers for each of them. Sometimes the answers may not make sense to us initially, but over time, God's truth always makes itself known.

Big Reveal #3

Whatever the goal, determine what success will take (cost), your capability to achieve it (budget), and the purpose behind it (ultimate or divine plan).

Helpful scriptures

"And anyone who does not carry his cross and follow me cannot be my disciple. Suppose one of you wants to build a tower. Will he not first sit down and estimate the cost to see if he has enough money to complete it? For if he lays the foundation and is not able to finish it, everyone who sees it will ridicule him, saying, 'This fellow began to build and was not able to finish.'"
Luke 14: 27-30 (NIV)

"By wisdom a house is built and through understanding it is established"
Proverbs 24:3 (NIV)

- 7 -

Choosing Wisely

Whether it is finding your dream house or finding Mr. or Mrs. Right, we are warned to choose wisely. Choosing wisely comprises prioritizing our *must haves*, counting up the costs (financial or emotional), and having the faith and perseverance to wait until the right choice has been revealed. When we place a high enough value on something we desire, we will continue to dream, hope, wait for, or pursue it until we find it. Only when we find it will we be satisfied. Sometimes we can lose patience and end up making compromises that go against what we once demanded. Choosing wisely demands that we remain steadfast and not compromise on those things that are at the very core of who we are, what we know, and what we believe. Nailing down what matters to us the most is the prerequisite work. I touched on this in the previous chapter about "Must Haves."

Making the right choices while pursuing one's "Dream Home" is crucial. Features such as fireplaces, basements, bonus rooms, pools, or hot tubs are just a few of the "extra" elements that exceed the homebuyers' basic requirements but can make or break their overall satisfaction with the property. At one point, a hot tub or spa was on my list of desired features for my dream home because of the benefits of relaxation. While searching for a property with a hot tub and researching having one installed, I learned there is quite a bit of maintenance that is required to enjoy its full benefits. As mentioned in the previous chapter, that required counting up the total costs for owning and regularly operating my beloved spa. For example, after adding water, the thermostat must be properly set for the water to reach the desired temperature. The amount of water and how the water is heated (electric or gas) will affect utility costs. You must also add chemicals to purify the water and prevent unwanted algae growth.

Over time, the routine maintenance required for your hot tub includes components such as the pump or water heater. These will fail when not maintained properly. A hot tub is a great feature to add to any home, but buyers must understand that there are costs associated with maintaining its benefits and usefulness. I would rather not have a hot tub at all than to have one that leaks, cannot heat the water to the desired temperature, or is filled with algae and other things that make it unpleasant. If you can't afford to maintain a hot tub, then it is probably not a good investment for you. This is a good example of why choosing wisely is so important. A good rule of thumb to follow is when you purchase or remodel a home, your personal net worth should increase because of your decision to do so. If your decision doesn't add value or worth, then it is probably not a good investment. Sometimes, the decision to buy or remodel a home may not initially appear to be a bad one until after the fact. Therefore, a careful inspection of a property along with an evaluation from a real estate advisor are always advised.

> If your decision doesn't add value or worth, then it is probably not a good investment.

RISKS

Risks are important to consider when faced with making a difficult choice or major decision, like buying a home. According to Merriam-Webster, *risk* describes the *possibility* of loss, injury, or peril. It also describes the chance that an investment will lose its value. We all incur some margin of risk every day in that we are exposed to the possibilities of danger and loss. Risk not only applies to the chance that a potential "bad thing" will happen, but it also describes our emotional state when faced with decisions that could cause that "bad thing" to maybe happen. Many studies focus on risk, particularly risk behaviors, risk tolerance, and risk personality types. Researchers have categorized, classified, and ranked risk in more ways than I care to outline. Besides, you are probably not reading this to become an expert in risk analysis and management. So instead of exploring that data in any great detail, I will simplify, or maybe even oversimplify, a small portion of some of the research on *risk* from a human behavior perspective. Here is my take on the topic of "Risk Personality Types."

I prefer to call them "Risk Taker Types." I believe that there are three main Risk Taker Types: (1) *Impulsive*, (2) *Moderate*, and (3) *Cautious*. Keep in mind that psychologists and other scientific researchers have identified seven or eight very distinct types. Whether you reference my three *Risk Taker Types,* or the seven or eight *Risk Personality Types* defined by leading behavioral scientists, "Risk Type" or better yet, our own "Risk Attitude" is a very important thing to figure out and understand about ourselves before making a big purchase or other major decision. It is also essential information to know and understand in both home-buying and relationships or marriage. So, let's explore them briefly.

First is the *Impulsive*. These are the folks who throw caution to the wind when pursuing their desires. They are often spontaneous, bold, and even reckless, and are not the least bit afraid of taking risks in situations that are considered both high risk and high reward. Next, are the *Moderate*. These are risk takers who can also be spontaneous like their impulsive counterparts however, they are rarely described as "reckless." They are mindful, thoughtful, balanced, and a little more cautious and calculated about the decisions they make or the projects they invest in. Although they may do a bit of research, they also rely on a kind of *gut instinct* when deciding. Last on my list is the *Cautious*. This group may have even started out as either "Impulsive" or "Moderate" but at some point, in their lives they became very conservative in their risk tolerance. I believe some people are born more *cautious* than others.

My daughter is a perfect example of this, she has been and still is extremely *cautious* about everything, from her first steps, to trying new foods, or going to new places, and even things like going to the doctor's or dentist's office for routine visits. I think she considers all new experiences *high risk* and as a result they are preceded by a careful testing of the waters, investigation, questioning, nervousness, and anxiety-ridden preparation (requiring lots of handholding and prayers). This extremely *cautious* attitude can result from a particularly painful or negative experience, but that is not always the case.

When I think about it, I have probably been all three types at different stages in my life. My advice to anyone faced with a decision, like a home purchase or some other major proposition, is to take a step back or a moment and realize that there is and will always be a measure of risk associated with every endeavor. We may never identify and mitigate all potential risks associated with a decision. Besides, we are mere humans. Even with the help of assisted technology, like some of the A.I. (Artificial Intelligence) tools that exist today, we can never fully predict and prepare for every possibility. History has taught us that as well prepared as we think we are, not even the engineers at NASA, or our best and brightest military leaders, can predict all of life's possibilities. One saving grace for people of faith that is that we have God on our side. There are many names for God, like Jehovah, Yahweh, the Creator, etc., but by whatever name you call Him, having God on your side mitigates all risk scenarios.

You can ask an "A.I. bot" any question and it will give a robust and comprehensive answer based on the sum of all the information it has access to. Not only can A.I. analyze data, but it also tries at predicting likelihood, a very good attempt. People of faith use prayer in the same or similar ways that some use technology. It is an additional powerful tool that can be used for every *Risk Taker Type*. Prayers help people make sense of their world, their homes, their relationships, and everything else concerning their lives. The belief is that there is a higher power that hears those prayers and offers direction toward the best possible resources and the best possible outcomes. If you are a believer, rely on your personal relationship with God to guide you in choosing wisely. God already knows you, what is best for you, and the plans He has for you.

- 8 -

Choosing Wisely

In real estate, there are always tons of possibilities to choose from in your desired location and price range. Sometimes, the house will have the right price, and sometimes even the right location, but the architectural style of the home or its layout may not be what you desire. Other times, the quality of construction or the overall condition of the property is of concern. But how does this all work when it is a dream relationship that we are seeking? We look at architectural style during our house hunting, but when looking at potential partners, we should consider lifestyle, quality of character, and the overall condition of a person's life. In both cases, choosing the right one does not happen by accident. Whether through trial and error, life experiences, careful inspection, passed-down instructions, wise counsel, or friendly advice, we figure out how to get the things that satisfy us the most and, conversely, how to avoid the things that do not. I believe we are continually learning and growing in this ability.

With dating, there may be "plenty of fish" in the sea, but not all of them will fit the criteria of what we desire. As mentioned in the first chapter, it is during childhood that our patterns of behavior and preferences are first formed. From the minute we are born until the current day, we can look back to see what has worked and what has not, and likewise, who has given us the greatest joy and who has not. It is the sum of all those experiences that help us with the relationship choices we ultimately make. When I look back over my life to identify my patterns and preferences, I am careful to not only recall the positive outcomes of the more successful choices, but I think that equally important to my life story are the missteps and mistakes made with my not-so-good choices. Regarding relationships, it is helpful to look at your *ex's* for clues.

My first relationship occurred while I was in college, my second was a post-college friendship that eventually blossomed into romance, and my last, but certainly not least, relationship has been with my husband. It sounds cliche, but it's nonetheless true that for me, the best was saved for last. What each of those relationships had in common was the incredible friendships that were shared. I never fell in love with anyone that I had not already fallen into friendship with. My definition of what makes a good friend was also my criteria of what makes an ideal mate. This probably explains why the men I dated casually, who were wonderful and seemed to have a lot going for them, never gained the prized "in a relationship" status with me. The truth is, we never made it to a "relationship" because they never graduated to my prerequisite "friend" status.

> My definition of what makes a good friend was also my criteria of what makes an ideal mate.

By the time I met my husband at age thirty-eight, I had learned a few things about myself. Besides knowing how important friendships were to me, I knew who I was and what I needed in a mate, despite being skeptical that I would ever find it. By this time, I had started to realize that my list of what I *didn't want* was becoming less and less of a factor. What you want and need is far more important than what you do not. No one goes to the grocery store with a list of things they *don't* want or need. My almost fatal flaw before then was that I had become overly cautious about choosing wisely. I was determined not to settle for anything less than perfection. It sounds like a good standard to have, the not settling part, but as I said I was "overly" cautious, which left me very guarded and somewhat emotionally unavailable. I was part "high standards" and part "fear and doubt". Thankfully, my faith kicked in at some point, helping me overcome the fear and doubt part.

Looking back to when I was a kid, I remember being at the local park or basketball court, playing with my potential kickball or basketball mates. Occasionally, I would have the privilege of picking my own team. I chose the ones who I felt had the best combination of skill and likeability. I picked kids who not only could help me win but also help me have fun doing it. This *choosing style* carried over into adolescence and adulthood. When I became the captain of my life's team, one of my greatest lessons learned was that my first pick should always be me. Prioritizing your own needs and desires is something that every adult should know how to do. After prioritizing me, I then pretty much "picked" the same way I did as a kid. I looked for people who had the skills and abilities that I lacked. They did not have to be doing better than me or have more to offer than me. In my mind, they simply needed to possess that thing(s) that I was missing. Being confident in my ability to win, I have also learned that no one wins alone.

Every successful person, organization, or team did not get there without the contributions of others. Therefore, I have never liked the phrase "pull yourself up by your bootstraps." It is misguided at best. Who provided the boots? And if you could buy them, by what means? Another thing I learned about myself was that I preferred to have fun while pursuing the win. I value having "playmates" and not just "teammates." Now please don't read any of this and make any conclusions about my success rate. People are all so incredibly different and amazingly unique.

> Being confident in my ability to win, I have also learned that no one wins alone.

Our human experiences affect us all differently. That means no two people are alike, not even biological twins. Thus, predicting success is a very difficult task. The good news is that with every choice comes valuable life lessons that improve one's likelihood of future success.

I learned through experience how to prioritize *my* dreams and desires and just how important that is to my overall happiness and well-being. I struggled with this for a while. It was because I was self-conscious and careful not to appear selfish in any way. Then I learned that making someone else's desires and dreams my priority usually left me feeling disappointed and unfulfilled. It eventually clicked, and I realized that another person's dreams or desires should never be more important than mine. Ideally, we should support and encourage each other in whatever dreams we both have. Lastly and probably most importantly, I learned the importance of *waiting for the right one*. Finding the right one or being found by the right one is wonderful indeed, but guess what? So is rejection, even though it doesn't feel as good.

One of my favorite affirmations goes something like this, "Man's rejection is God's protection." It really resonated with me the first time I heard it because it helped me make sense of those times when I felt like I did everything right but still didn't get the outcome I was hoping for. I discovered that it was far better to have someone who sees and knows your value than to try to convince them of how happy they would be if they picked you to join their team. A "Pick-Me-Girl" comes to mind. I didn't know what that was until my daughter explained it one day. Urban dictionary describes it as this:

"Pick-Me-Girl" (noun, slang, derogatory);
a woman who asserts that she is unlike (and sometimes
better than) most other women in order to gain attention,
approval, or validation from men.

I am a lot of things, but I am nobody's "Pick-Me-Girl!" I am also one of those who firmly believe that "good things come to those who wait." Of course, working on becoming your "best self" while you wait is paramount.

My husband and I met and fell in love during a time of great personal conflict and grief for him. A failed marriage and another subsequent failed relationship had taken its toll on him. As for me, I was at a crossroads in life, trying to decide whether I would choose to be in a permanent state of emotional withdrawal or allow God to take the reins. I trusted God with my spirit, but could He be trusted with my relationships? I mean, what if He decided that who I liked the most was not His choice for me? To trust or not to trust was my dilemma. In a sense, my husband and I were both at the same crossroads. We both had some major decisions to make.

According to my calculations, the risk of disappointment, heartbreak, and loss seemed high when I considered him as a potential mate. In fact, the stakes were high for both of us. I had to make the ultimate decision of whether to allow a friendship to grow or to run for the hills! I had a strong feeling that allowing a friendship to develop would change my life trajectory dramatically, for better or worse. I was right, it did! At first, At first I didn't think he possessed the "architectural style" that I was usually drawn to, but he was like stumbling upon a charming bungalow that needed a little TLC because of neglect or lack of maintenance. I could see past all of that and knew in my gut that he had "good bones." Prior to running into my husband, also known as the "charming fixer," I admittedly found myself distracted by men who were likened to homes with fancy facades and "high-end" finishes, only to be disappointed to find poor craftsmanship or flawed foundations underneath. It told myself that if this time were to be different, I would have to see with fresh eyes. I prayed. I was desperate to choose wisely this time around.

Our friendship developed slowly. Realizing what was at stake, I knew I had some decisions to make. It was the same type of decision as when you think that you have found that perfect home. Somewhere amid all the excitement, there is a sobering moment where you ask yourself questions like, *Is this what I really want? Should I consider other options?*

Is this a good and sound investment of my resources? A compulsion came over me, insisting that I take a risk and stay the course this time rather than doing what I normally did. No more choking my feelings out, leaving them to die prematurely to avoid disappointment. I remember asking myself some of those same familiar questions, *"Is this what I really want?"* and *"Does this have the potential to be a good investment?"*

At the beginning of us, I remember intentionally trying to keep things from progressing too fast, but a wonderful friendship developed and started to grow, and a strong connection emerged. After getting to know each other, it was clear that our emotional, spiritual and physical attraction for each other was flourishing. Our friendship continued to grow, as did our mutual affection and admiration for one another. Then it hit me. Whether I was ready for it or not, we were both falling very much in love. It was like a sun shower, rain suddenly appearing from sunny skies, gently replenishing the dry and thirsty ground. We were wildflowers soaking up the unexpected water that caused our petals to open and stretch toward the sky. The timing was perfect because, before our first date, we both had started to wither in our respective dry places.

When my husband reflects on our beginnings, he often asserts that he chose me at first glance. That may be true, but it took longer for me. As I mentioned before, I was overly cautious and careful with my evaluation of people. Then I remembered the importance of faith and prayer, especially when faced with big life decisions. Whether you are Christian, Jewish, Muslim, or Hindu, faith has always been a key differentiator of long-term success and fulfillment. So, I fervently asked God to reveal what His right choice was for me. An answer came, but not quickly. I had to wait for it patiently. It trickled in, in multiple times and ways, each time confirming what I believed and feared simultaneously. God was saying "yes" that my future husband was indeed the chosen one for me. I could give my heart permission to accept my husband's offer of "forever." Thankfully, I believe we both choose wisely as we continue to love and grow and work together towards making our dreams a reality every day.

Big Reveal #4

Careful examination coupled with godly wisdom helps you make good decisions and achieve the best possible outcomes.

Helpful Scriptures

"Trust in the LORD with all your heart; do not depend on your own understanding. Seek his will in all you do, and he will show you which path to take."
Proverbs 3:5-6 (NLT)

"But if any of you lacks wisdom, let him ask of God, who gives to all generously and without reproach, and it will be given to him."
James 1:5 (NASB)

"The instruction of the wise is like a life-giving fountain; those who accept it avoid the snares of death."
Proverbs 13:14 (NLT)

- 9 -

Contingencies with Confidence

Once you have explored your options, reviewed your *must-haves*, counted up the cost for what you desire, and made your wise home choice, it is important to evaluate how much insurance coverage you will need. Notice I did not say decide if you want to get insurance. Unfortunately, acquiring insurance for an investment like a new house is rarely ever "optional." Many people take my husband's stance, which is "Home Insurance is a complete SCAM!" He says this because insurance rates keep going up, especially in the States prone to natural disasters, but the insurance companies are covering less and less. You will probably pay premiums for years for something you may never use. Nonetheless, it is still something I consider a necessary evil. Why? Insurance is a means of protection from financial loss because of any number of unforeseen specified events or circumstances. It is a type of guarantee against loss or harm. In fact, insurance products are sold to mitigate the risk of loss in almost every area of our existence. For example, there is health insurance to guarantee payments for medical services, there is car insurance to guarantee payments to cover damages to your vehicle, travel insurance to recover payment for trip disruptions or cancelations, and of course property insurance to guarantee payments to cover your home and its contents in the case of a loss event.

People ensure many things of value because it gives the assurance that when the unpredictable happens, they will be able to recover from it without suffering severe or catastrophic financial consequences. I would venture to say that everyone we know is currently covered by some kind of insurance. Homeowners, renters, health, life, disability, auto, workman's comp, or even third-party liability coverage, to name a few. Even if we never use it, the coverage is there to offer vital help when something bad happens. The reason we even have an insurance industry is that, based on past experiences, we can predict the likelihood of and calculate the risk for specific bad things. Insurance became the mechanism for providing recovery and provision if those specific bad things ever occurred. Whether you are buying a new home or getting some major renovations done, having the right amount and the right type of insurance is crucial. After completing a renovation project that increases the value of your home, your insurance coverage should also be updated to reflect those upgrades.

We have talked about the importance of having adequate insurance for your new home purchase, but what about reno projects? It is equally important to ensure you have sufficient coverage during a major renovation project. There are a lot more risks to consider when you hire a contractor who will likely hire subcontractors to do work in your home. It is common practice for contractors vying for your business to entice you with beautiful before and after photos, product samples, and special promotional rates or savings if you book the job by some soon-approaching date. It is so easy to get caught up in envisioning all the desires you have for your home coming to fruition; however, one of the most essential considerations you can have before kicking off your project is whether your current insurance covers your contractor and then making sure that your contractor has their own insurance coverage as part of their contract.

Do the proper due diligence and hire a *good* contractor to do work in your home. This is more than a mere suggestion or helpful hint. The best contractors are licensed AND insured. This is one of my general rules, and it is as important, if not more so, than the countertops, flooring, backsplash, or other options that are available for your new kitchen or bath. Here's a *Pro-tip*: Asking for previous customer references in addition to your contractor's proof of insurance. Another *Pro-tip* is to make sure their coverage dates are current, and the coverage amounts for your contractor's insurance are adequate. Depending on the size of the project, you may also want to consider increasing the liability coverage on your own existing insurance policy or possibly even getting a separate policy to cover any gaps.

> The best contractors are licensed AND insured.

Keep in mind that it does not matter if you are planning to hire a contractor for a big project or use skilled day laborers for smaller jobs, the liability coverage on your homeowner's policy will cover bodily injury and property damage sustained by others. Larger projects requiring several types of contractors (i.e., electrical, plumbing, HVAC, etc.) have increased risk and thus require increased coverage. When in doubt, it is always a good idea to contact your insurance agent to discuss your current coverage limits, being sure to discuss the details and budget for your upcoming project.

After your project is complete, make sure the value of your improvements in relation to the value of your home is included in your total coverage. Both market value and replacement costs are affected by home improvements. Even smaller projects can impact the total cost of rebuilding your home in the case of a total loss. The marble or quartz you upgrade to can be more expensive to replace than the original builder-grade materials. Some improvements can reduce the cost of your homeowner's coverage. Things like storm windows, doors or roof replacements usually qualify for discounts on your existing coverage. Be proactive and contact your insurance agent to discuss your plans before time.

How it provides provision after the occurrence of unforeseen events and damages makes insurance a type of "contingency" reserve. A contingency is a future event or circumstance which is possible but cannot be predicted with certainty. The contingency budget is a way to set aside provisions for any unforeseen events or circumstances. For the property owner doing a remodeling project, it is recommended that as much as 15% of the total reno budget be held back for unforeseen incidental expenses. Some of those unscheduled and unplanned emergencies may include electrical issues, foundation or structural issues, asbestos, lead, or other hazardous materials that require mediation. Sometimes environmental issues, such as pests or even unstable ground conditions, are revealed. Contingency reserves help resolve some of those issues so the project can move forward toward completion.

- 10 -

Contingencies with Confidence

Contingency is a simple concept to grasp when referring to construction, but what about relationships? Can you, or should you, establish contingency reserves for your committed relationships? It is not so easy or pragmatic to plan for unforeseen emotional challenges. It's impossible to reserve 15% of your love and positive emotions solely for major conflicts. It certainly is not practical or moral to have outside persons on "standby" just in case things don't work out. Having a "side piece," waiting in the wings if your relationship hits a bump in the road is a sure-fire way to ensure that your relationship will never reach its fullest potential. So, what can we do? How do we plan for the unexpected issues that may come up in our marriages? I believe that there is a type of relationship contingency reserve that we all can create.

A relationship contingency reserve comprises things like identifying people who are invested in the success of the

> I believe that there is a type of relationship contingency reserve that we all can create.

relationship. These same people are later used as needed, as a source of encouragement and advice during challenging times. A relationship contingency reserve may also include things like access to marriage and family counseling services. Counseling professionals help to maintain or redirect the relationship to the desired course. People of faith have additional options. People can find answers and needed relationship help in the scriptures. When I refer to scriptures, I hope to draw a contrast between well intentioned written works inspired by "self-help" gurus and the revered texts regarded as having been inspired by the Creator God. Holy scriptures represent the testimony of God to mankind and the serve as guidebooks for humanity. Reading and studying God's testimonies helps to prepare us for the things we are likely to experience in life. For example, the Bible recounts many stories of tragedy, relationship problems, disasters, and moral dilemmas that people faced throughout history.

In all those stories, the one thing they have in common is a loving God providing both refuge and remedies. For example, when catastrophic rains were approaching, threatening the lives of Noah, his family and all of God's creation, God gave Noah instructions to build a huge rescue boat called an "ark". In another story, severe drought and famine were approaching, threatening the lives of hundreds of thousands. God created a "contingency plan" for this by sending Joseph, a dreamer with a fancy coat, to Egypt, allowing him to be promoted to a role that helped save his family, Israel, and other nations in that region. Another example is the story of Lot. According to the Bible, Lot was the nephew of Abram (Abraham). He and his wife were forced to be separated from his Uncle Abram and his wife. They were all on the move because of a lack of resources where they lived. Lot and his wife ended up settling a little piece of land near a town called Sodom while his Uncle Abram continued on to eventually settle in a land called Canaan. The Bible describes the men of Lot's new neighborhood Sodom as "wicked, and great sinners against the Lord," Genesis 13:13.

As the story goes, God sent two angels in the form of men to warn Lot that the land of Sodom and nearby Gomorrah would be destroyed.

The angels instructed Lot to pack up his family and leave Sodom. Most importantly, the angels warned him not to stop to look back toward the land that God was about to destroy. While on their way out of the doomed city, Lot's wife glanced back to see the destruction. This was clearly against the angel's instructions and, as a result, the story says that she immediately turned into a pillar of salt. This and all the other stories paint a picture of God's relationship with humanity. He never prevents us from making our own life choices. Instead, God presents to us His plans, which serve as a blueprint for a purposeful and abundant life.

If we look at insurance in the context of relationships, we will not find any products. The closest example to insurance that I can think of is legal protection that some couples choose to use before they get married called a "pre-nuptial agreement," but even that is insufficient in protecting both parties from all the tangible and intangible losses that occur as the result of separation and divorce. An untapped gold mine for investors would surely be the business of creating insurance products that could help mitigate the pain and suffering caused by relationships that have gone bad. Can you imagine calling up "Jake from State Farm" to get rates on policies to protect against chronic cheating, "can't-keep-a-job syndrome," or severe jealousy?

When my husband and I started dating, we had no insurance policy to protect our hearts from potential loss. I probably would have bought one if there were such a thing. Especially after finding out that he had a history of infidelity and some serious insecurities. I was also a piece of work with my history of commitment issues and unrealistic expectations. How on earth could a successful relationship be built under those circumstances? What were the odds that we could construct a healthy relationship where we could meet each other's needs while increasing our value? Insurance is a means of protecting oneself against loss or harm because of many

> When my husband and I started dating, we had no insurance policy to protect our hearts from potential loss.

specified events or circumstances. Since there are no insurance products or guarantees for matters of the heart, there was something that helped to reassure us and give us a bit of confidence. My husband and I were then and still are believers, people of faith. We share the same faith, which is the gospel of Christ or Christianity. Being Christians was not a guarantee that we would make it. In fact, half of Christian marriages end in divorce. It just meant that we both believed in a higher power who could help us overcome everything and keep us together. We would still have to experience all the conflicts, money issues, insecurities, family drama, and other typical issues that all couples face. The difference, however, was that we placed our confidence in a God with a track record of *unbroken* promises who constantly gives us hope for a bright future. With a little bit of faith, we believed God would see us through every adversity we could imagine and that our marriage would flourish until death.

Initially, I had very little confidence that my husband and I could make the distance, given our combined issues, but because of our faith, we both hung our hopes on what God could do instead of what we could not do. We believed He was going to do something great through us. God already had a proven track record for doing awesome, amazing, unlikely, improbable, impossible, and other extraordinary things through ordinary people.

Finding the right mate can be like finding the right contractor for your renovation project. "Insurance" is a requirement for any contractor I choose. Likewise, God's "assurance" was a requirement for any life partner I choose.

Big Reveal #5

During the purchase of your dream home or at the beginning of a major renovation or committed relationship, you should identify and secure any protections that are available so that you can move forward with confidence.

Helpful scriptures:

Let us then with confidence draw near to the throne of grace, that we may receive mercy and find grace to help in time of need," Hebrews 4:16 (ESV)

"For the Lord will be your confidence and will keep your foot from being caught," Proverbs 3:26 (ESV)

"In the fear of the Lord one has strong confidence, and his children will have a refuge," Proverbs 14:26 (ESV)

"And we know that for those who love God all things work together for good, for those who are called according to his purpose," Romans 8:28 (ESV)

- 11 -

A Masterful Design

Throughout history, there have been many stories of great things being built under near-impossible circumstances and with very limited resources. This list includes things like bridges, castles, towers, railroads, and dams. For example, the Great Wall in China is a network of barrier fortifications built using only local resources like stone, dirt, and wood. Different Chinese rulers built it over a 2000-year period to protect China's northern borders, and it is still intact today. Other structures, which are recognized as some of the "Great Wonders of the World," include the Great Pyramid of Giza, which is a tomb for one of the Egyptian pharaohs. This famous structure in Egypt held the title as the tallest manmade structure for over 3800 years. Other great structures include the Colosseum in Rome, which once held the title of the largest amphitheater, and the famous and multipurpose Acropolis in Greece, which has served as a citadel, a mythical home for gods and a religious center for different faiths.

During modern times, there has been a rise in impressive architectural feats of wonder like the Golden Gate Bridge, the Oculus in New York City, and the Burj Khalifa in Dubai. The Bible recounts other examples of great builds. Noah built the Arc and Solomon built the Temple Mount, to name just a few. All these examples started as ideas, and when placed in the hands of masterful architects and builders, the results were extraordinary. Every person has an idea, a dream, or preference concerning their new home, whether it is for new construction, an existing building, or a remodel. In each case, an architect, builder, and/or general contractor have been or will be required to make the dream a reality.

I consider my current home my "dream home" but it probably will not appear in any magazines. It is an attached townhouse, one of four in our section and part of one of those planned communities, complete with community pools, boat docks, and a dedicated fishing dock. From the outside, our three-story unit is indistinguishable from the other units in our row. We live in a quiet, "Key West" style, village themed community located alongside intercostal waters on the west coast of central Florida. Our home is approximately one mile from the Gulf of Mexico. One of our primary criteria for choosing this home was location. Before we considered things like architecture style, interior design, or community amenities, we had already decided where our new house should be. For us (mainly me), the beach has always been my ultimate location. Growing up on the South Carolina coast, there was always a body of water within a couple of minutes from me. Bridges had to be crossed to get to most places. Fishing, crabbing, swimming, and just gazing at the many boats and glistening waterways have been some of my favorite pastimes as far back as I can remember. The smell of salt marshes and the sight of shrimp boats give me a strange feeling of being free, while being very connected to and dependent on my surroundings.

As a result, my experiences living in land-locked places have been short-lived. The connection I feel to the ocean and other waterways is strong. This was not something my husband and I shared when we met, but over time, he has adapted to it. We both now have what I call "water-lust." Just like wanderlust, that strong desire to travel (which I also have), my husband and I have a strong desire to be near the water. Water for me includes ponds, lakes, rivers, bays, inlets, intercostal areas, but most of all, oceans and seas. So, the search for our dream home started with the location we passionately felt compelled to be. That passion became a dream, the dream became a vision, the vision became a plan, and that plan became our reality.

Discovering the perfect location for your forever home is crucial. Some people know it right away, while others take months or even years to figure it out. It is important to take the time to scout out different locations to determine whether they fulfill both the practical and emotional needs that come with finding "home." A point of distinction I suggest, is searching for a house versus searching for a home. To me, those are two different goals. A house is a place of lodging where you establish residency. It is a structure where your personal belongings are stored, and where you live out your daily existence. A home, on the other hand, particularly a "forever home" is that place where one lives out one's dreams, desires, and purpose. It is a place of nurturing where a sense of security and peace make up the foundation. This is why finding the right builder is so important.

> A point of distinction I suggest, is searching for a house versus searching for a home.

Let's explore the role of the builder regarding your dream home search. When exploring the inventory of existing homes for sale, you may find references to the builder in the MLS description. For example, during one of our previous home searches, we looked at the listings for homes in the specific neighborhood that we were interested in. It was interesting to see that some of the property descriptions began with the name of the builder before describing the features of the home. The listing would say, "Charles Rutenberg built home in the desirable XYZ neighborhood." Once we checked out a few of the homes built by this builder, we understood why his name was so prominent in the property description. These *Rutenberg-built* homes have stood the test of time. They are homes built with quality materials, with unique architectural features such as cedar ceiling beams and stone fireplace surrounds. They tended to be larger custom homes with semi-open floor plans, efficient use of space, tons of storage, and design elements that integrated and featured what the location offered. Courtyards and atriums that showcased native plants and custom pools with screened lanais to complement the outdoor living that the area is known for. Cypress, mahogany, and rich oak hardwoods were used instead of cheaper options. These homes were solid, meeting the highest building standards.

Even though we never met this builder or worked with him personally, we had a pretty good idea of what we could expect from his workmanship. We saw homes that had been tested and proven, having survived some of the harshest tropical weather conditions. A wise and reputable builder should spare no expense in ensuring that the foundation and footings of their projects have structural integrity and are as incorruptible as possible.

Although my husband and I have never taken on a new construction project in our quest to find the perfect home, the lessons we learned about finding the right builder still hold true. For example, if we had found an ideal lot in our most desired location. The second most important decision, after the lot's location, was selecting the best builder for the job. We would use four basic criteria to help us make that determination:

- *capability*
- *compatibility*
- *reliability*
- *accountability*.

First, we consider the builders' *capability*. This refers to a builder's ability to do the job. Education and training, licenses and certifications, and registrations with well-known professional business organizations are a few criteria that can be used to determine your builder's capability. In fact, the very designation as a "master builder" is a noteworthy clue. The qualifications for a "master builder" as compared to a "general contractor" are very distinct and set one apart from the other. I would liken it to the difference between a "specialist" versus a "general practitioner" in the medical field. In the construction world, there are tradesmen, and there are "master tradesmen." Likewise, a carpenter differs vastly from a builder. In all these cases, it is implied that all possess skills in their respective fields, but the term "master" describes someone who is masterful, meaning they have become a very skilled and proficient expert at something.

There are some assumptions that can be made about "master builders." This includes an expectation that they comply with all the relevant laws, codes, and regulations that apply to the building industry; that they actively and continually improve the skills they have; they are fair in all their dealings with clients and other professionals; and finally, they act with integrity. "How capable is (for new builds) or was (for existing homes) the builder?" is the bottom-line question here. Once you establish capability, then *compatibility* is the next most important factor to consider. When two or more parties go into contract or agreement with one another intending to create some shared vision together, the probability of success depends on how well they get along. Compatibility refers to more than the same personality. Let me switch to the example of couples since that is usually the place where emphasis is often placed on this notion of compatibility.

In the previous chapter about "Must Haves," I said, "*Spiritual compatibility and spiritual maturity are key concepts that absolutely must be explored before you commit yourself to another.*" Building on that, overall compatibility is imperative. Compatibility refers to having both empathy and affinity for the other party. People who are compatible have similar or the same mindset about things. They have a rapport when they communicate because they have mutual regard and admiration for each other. They are more likely to put extra effort into creating a harmonious and agreeable experience. For example, if timelines and adhering to schedules is important to one party, then the other party will respectfully comply with that expectation because of their mutual regard for one another.

Compatibility can be a great predictor of future outcomes. It also explains how a rigid taskmaster and a laid-back creative person can build something beautiful together. Although they are different, they can also be compatible. The next criterion for selecting the right builder is *reliability*. Some due diligence is required for this one. Your personality will dictate how far to take this, but it is highly recommended that you do a little research on the reputation of the builder in question. How successful were they in previous projects? How well do their builds hold up over time? How satisfied were their clients with the results?

> Compatibility can be a great predictor of future outcomes.

What is their rating with organizations like the Better Business Bureau or even YELP? The information you find is useful, whether you are building a new home or buying an existing one.

During the mid-2000s, there was a housing boom in central and south Florida in which tons of new developments were being built within popular metro areas and there was a dozen or more builders leading most of these projects. Some of those builders had a strong reputation and a long history in Florida. Some were nationally known, but new to the area, and others were new to the scene altogether. After about seven to ten years had passed, these newly built homes told the builder's story. Defective drywall products, premature wear, and deterioration of everything from paint to tile work, cracks in exterior stucco walls, and, in these worse examples, structural or foundation issues appeared. Most buyers during that boom were distracted by attractive financial incentives or tempted by modern finishes and appliance packages. For the builders that were new to the area, a quick search of the Better Business Bureau complaints may have helped predict some of these potential problems.

Today, there are a lot of websites that offer online reviews of products and services. You may feel that it is too much information to sift through, but in doing so, you could avoid making a bad choice. You can also ask the builder or contractor for customer and professional references. Wherever possible, talk to someone who has already had experience with the builder you are considering. Do they have a website? Does it have any reviews posted? How detailed are the reviews? Real reviews from real customers do not sound like commercial soundbites. *Reliability* refers to trustworthiness, integrity, accuracy, authenticity, and safety. How *reliable* is the master builder?

The final criterion is *accountability*. When it comes to the services you want to contract for, *accountability* refers mostly to legal liability. That means a person or entity takes full legal responsibility if something goes wrong and then they take every provision to right the wrong. There is special coverage called liability insurance that your builder should possess in an amount that covers your risk. Don't be afraid to ask questions. You are not being "nosey" or "intrusive" when you ask for copies of their COI (Certificates of Insurance). Of course, you can assume that a builder or contractor's insurance coverage is adequate and up to date, but then who wants to take the risk of being wrong, especially when you don't have to? You can determine *accountability* by taking a closer look at the steps a person has taken to protect themselves and others from everything they are responsible for.

- 12 -

A Masterful Design

There has been a dual application for the truths I have shared so far. They have applied to both real estate and relationships. You should not be surprised to hear from me that the criterion for selecting the right builder also applies to relationships. In relationships, we all ultimately want someone who can love us, be *compatible* with us, *reliable* concerning us, and *accountable* to us. It takes time, investigation, observation, and personal reflection to make informed judgments about the people in our lives. Too often, we assign major roles to people who are not equipped or prepared to handle them.

When she was younger, our daughter liked to help in the kitchen when my husband or I cooked. She enjoyed it so much that she even joined a kid's cooking club at her elementary school. I remember when my husband and I were asked to host a special event in our home, my daughter volunteered to handle all the cooking. Although I cheered her good intentions, enthusiasm, and fearless optimism, I politely let her know it was too big of a job for her to handle. My response was based on my personal knowledge and experience concerning her capability, reliability, and accountability. She did, however, have compatibility working in her favor. She knew exactly what foods we enjoyed, and we all had fun together in the kitchen, enjoying both the process and the finished product.

Unfortunately, compatibility alone falls short of what is ultimately needed for success in long-term committed relationships. In hindsight, I can see that during my courtship with my husband, I was quietly evaluating the criteria suggested for builders (capability, compatibility, reliability, and accountability). Perhaps he was subconsciously evaluating those same things in me. Building a successful marriage with someone is no small feat, so it is important to know as much as possible about who you are building with. Some people rely too heavily on the "good vibes" or "positive energy" they feel during the initial stages. Funny thing about feelings, they almost always eventually change or fail at some point. When falling in love with someone, the feelings you experience are so intense and powerful that it's difficult to think clearly. If you are considering making the commitment to marry, understand that your love for each other will not be enough to build something strong and beautiful that will stand the tests of time.

I remember reading and hearing that "God knew us before we were born." That phrase comes from a scripture in the Bible. It did not quite make sense to me when I first heard it, but as I matured, I realized what it meant. I believe it means that God created each of us with very specific ideas and plans in mind. Some refer to it as *your purpose,* but it stretches beyond that. Purpose answers the question of "why?" The notion of God knowing us before we were born answers not just the "why" but also the "when," "where," "what," and the "how" of our existence. The one thing that most religions agree upon is the notion that God always has a vision and an intention for everything He creates. This includes people and every other living thing in nature. I believe that in God's vision for people, he gives each of us unique gifts, abilities, talents, interests, and passions. If we make it past the trauma of birth, these things are then cultivated throughout our lives through different experiences. Here is an example of how this played out in my life.

I was born to a widowed mother in a coastal town. I later moved away to a landlocked city and matured through my many experiences. After slowly becoming dissatisfied with my surroundings, a vacation took me to the Gulf Coast of Florida. That trip ignited my longing to be near water. This resulted in a subsequent relocation to Florida, which became my ultimate desired location for everything else I set out to do. After some years in Florida, I had to move to the Northeast for work. Ultimately, I felt strongly compelled to move back to Florida some five years later. During my five years away from Florida, I discovered my joy and passion for writing. Upon my return, I reconnected with some of my dearest friends, and met some new ones, including my future husband. Not long afterwards, my life was forever changed. I got married, started a family, discovered my purpose, found my dream home, and so much more. I believe there was and continues to be a Master Builder at work in my life, making everything work together perfectly.

In summary, the takeaway is that physical structures are not the only things built by Master Builders. People are, too. Marriage is also part of God's divine design. Before my husband and I met each other, we had good jobs and were in good health. Separately, we could have continued to live our respective lives and be relatively happy. From society's standards, we were doing okay, and to some, we were doing better than okay. God had already blessed us in so many ways before our coming together. However, since our coming together and subsequent marriage, we have seen ourselves grow significantly (mentally, emotionally, spiritually, and financially), and we have made a far greater impact as a married couple than either of us had ever made on our own. Some results of our growth include the purchase of our dream home(s), the launch of a successful landscaping business, and dedicating ourselves to ministry

> Marriage is also part of God's divine design.

service. We also experienced the birth of our daughter, the addition of a new daughter-in-law, grandchildren, plus our circle of family and friends has continued to grow. Who can tell where our separate paths would have led us? God has built a beautiful family and a successful business and allowed us to obtain our forever home in one of our favorite coastal communities. We routinely travel throughout the US and abroad, causing our circle of influence to continue to grow. God took our individual talents, strengths, and passions and then put us together to build something lasting and great! We are a legacy and a testament to God's workmanship as the "Master Builder" of our lives. A master builder is defined as *someone who is skilled in the art of building also an architect."* An architect designs, makes, and/or supervises the construction of their design. It takes a master builder, working with good quality materials (previously tested and proven), a solid foundation, and masterful workmanship to build something lasting and great. Whatever the project, please ensure that the right master builder is engaged. The finished product stands as a testament to the builder.

Big Reveal #6

Before taking on a new build, purchasing an existing home, or building your dream marriage, get to know the builder so you may have confidence and trust in their creation.

Helpful Scriptures

"Unless the LORD builds the house, they labor in vain who build it; Unless the LORD guards the city, The watchman keeps awake in vain,"
Psalms 127:1 (ESV)

"For every house is built by someone, but God is the builder of everything,"
Hebrews 3:4 (ESV)

- 13 -

From Permits to Finished Product

When searching for the perfect house to make into your dream home, some buyers will opt for new construction that they can customize according to their design preferences to make their own. Other buyers prefer to find an existing build that they can remodel and mold into their idea of perfection. Occasionally buyers will find an existing home that comes close to meeting their ultimate criteria, but even then, renovations are likely sometime down the road. Almost all construction and renovation projects require a building permit. A building permit is an official approval issued by a local government agency that allows someone to proceed with a construction or remodeling project on their property. The purpose of the permit is to ensure that the project plans comply with local standards for land use, zoning, and construction codes that comply with current recommended installation practices. These standards should ensure

the safety of current and future occupants and provide enforcement of
zoning and land-use policies. Some areas the building permit process
may address include the structural integrity of the framing work, the
foundation, roofs, windows, zoning, sanitation, water, sewer lines, fire
protection, HVAC, electrical service, and even environmental impact.

Most people agree (in principle at least) with the necessity of
getting the proper permits. However, complaints usually come after
learning how much additional cost and time comes with this process.
For some, the added time and expense of getting the required permits
outweigh the risk of not having them. Much to their surprise, these
same folks will often learn the hard way about the financial and legal
consequences of not getting the proper authorizations. Local permitting
requirements are challenging for those personality types who dislike
anyone telling them what to do or how to do it. Whether or not you
like it, someone in authority must grant you permission to build or
to proceed with what you may have already started building on your
own without prior permission.

The word *permit* is derived from the word permission, which means
formal consent or being given the authorization to do something. When
a permit is received, it means you have been given the authorization,
the right, the license, the power, the consent, the thumbs up, or the
blessing to proceed. On the flip side, if you are the issuer of a permit,
you are authorizing, granting, licensing, empowering, consenting, and
giving the blessing for someone else to proceed. *Permits* are granted
all the time, formally, as with building projects or with beginner
drivers, and informally, like within relationships of all kinds. Children
must get *permission* from their parents before they may do certain
things or go to certain places. Women and men both give and receive
permits when they date, which is why it is so important for everyone
to understand who is in authority of what and why. With this, we can
appreciate the benefits of getting the proper permits and understand
the consequences of moving ahead without one.

It, unfortunately, is common for homeowners to complete some
home improvement projects without applying for a permit, paying the

application fee, or having the work properly inspected and approved. While it is possible that such projects can be completed successfully and never cause problems, it is not good practice to bypass the official permitting process. Here are some examples of the consequences of not getting properly permitted:

1. *If or when you try to sell your house, the buyers' inspection may uncover remodeling or additions that were done without proper permits, and which may not be completely up to code. This can prevent you from selling the house and may require that you undo the previous work and start again—this time with a permit.*

2. *In the event of a fire, structural collapse, or major plumbing problem, if it is discovered the mishap results from work that was done without the benefit of a permit or inspections, it is possible that your homeowner's liability insurance policy may decline to cover the damage. The permit is the authority and permission to proceed based on very specific requirements and best practices that ensure current and future safety.*

Remodeling projects almost always require some sort of demolition work prior to the installation of the addition or modification of existing infrastructure. There is a tearing down that is required before the building up. In every building scenario, there are areas that may need to be torn down and removed before something new and more desirable can be built. For new builds, there is less demand for demo, but it may still be required at some point along the way. The demolition work on construction sites can be considered the most essential part of the project. Although more emphasis is placed on other skilled labor roles such as plumber, electrician, carpentry, HVAC tech, bricklayer, landscape architect, etc., the demolition workers are the true unsung heroes in the construction field.

For new builds, demo may include tearing down and removing pre-existing unsound structures that exist on the site, or clearing debris (site prep), to make sure the job site is safe and ready for new construction work. For remodeling projects in existing homes, the demo work serves much of the same purpose as with new builds. It involves destroying and removing any undesired fixtures or structures to prepare for the installation of new ones. The demolition work for remodeling projects includes things like the destruction and removal of undesired cabinetry, ugly kitchen or bath fixtures, unflattering flooring, walls, ceilings, essentially any and everything that is no longer wanted and is scheduled to be rebuilt or replaced. Demolition ranges in complexity from project to project. It can go from what I would describe as cosmetic demolition (a simple tear out), to other more structural examples. Cosmetic demolition involves tearing down or removing something based on its outward appearance. For example, ugly floor tiles, linoleum, or shag carpeting are things that grab your attention first when you enter a home, so they are the first to be removed. You may miss the updates to light fixtures, or new furniture, or the newly remodeled kitchen if you have to walk across ugly flooring to get there. Likewise, unsightly wallpaper is also a scene stealer. The reverse is also true. Who cares how great the new floors look in a kitchen when the appliances are old, the sinks are chipped or rusted, and the fluorescent ceiling light cluster is cracked and yellowing?

Cosmetic demolition tears down and removes the unsightly things that are visible. Other things that are not as visible to the naked eye must also be taken out before something new can be built on or around it. These are structural things, architectural things, and things that carry a load. This type of demolition should not be approached with random brute force, but instead through careful calculation and intentional actions that will yield a predictable outcome. For example, some projects require bearing load-bearing walls to be removed, others may require roofs, windows, chimneys, or even whole foundation entire foundations to be dismantled. A special set of skills and qualifications are required when something carries a load, whether it is a window, a door, a wall, a roof, or a concrete foundation slab. Special building permits must be applied for and issued to complete this type of work. *Structural integrity* refers to the ability of something to hold together under the stress of a heavy load. Bridges, buildings, statues, and monuments are all things that must have structural integrity.

When examining your dream home, remember that the overall value of any new or existing home is determined by its location and the quality of its construction. A building must be architecturally sound and the construction or building materials must be of a certain standard. Nobody wants to move into a home whose plans were not designed by a licensed architect using building materials that are poorly rated and worse than that, poorly installed. Since architecture was already covered in the Master Builder chapter, let us now explore the basic building blocks of any sound home or structure that determine the building's structural integrity. No matter the type of home you prefer (ranch, two-story, colonial, modern, craftsman, farmhouse, townhouse, row house, condo, or loft), they all have several key elements in common. They can all be built using many materials, but each one must have a foundation, a roof, windows, and doors. You cannot start a new build or major remodel without first considering these elements.

> *Structural integrity refers to the ability of something to hold together under the stress of a heavy load.*

There are strict building codes that govern and control how these elements are installed and what materials can be used. New builds are a clean slate. Builders meet regularly with homeowners to review the project plans and progress throughout the build. There is continuity throughout this process because there is one general contractor controlling the project from beginning to end. In working with an existing home, your remodel plans must be compatible with the original build. Major components of a house like masonry, framing (from walls to roof), and even windows and doors are things that your remodel plans may affect. Some elements require unique skilled laborers. Masonry is one of them. Masonry materials consist of stone, clay, brick, or concrete. The foundation of any sound building is probably made from masonry materials, not just in modern times, but from all the way back to the beginning of time.

Ancient structures in Africa, Europe, South America, and Asia that archaeologists have discovered and preserved are made from masonry materials. Houses of worship have a common history, from ancient temples and mosques to modern-day churches and cathedrals, of being built on some type of stone foundation. In biblical times, the term "cornerstone" was used to describe the initial stone slab on which a building was constructed. The temple would be built on this large foundational slab, and the rest of the building would be constructed around it, conforming to all its angles. Most of the time, both interior and exterior elements were made from masonry such as stone. Unless the outside of the building is made from brick or stone, the masonry that is in that building will often be overlooked because it is hidden. My Florida home's exterior is vinyl, faux-wood siding, but that siding is covering up foundational walls made with concrete cinder blocks. The masonry is hidden, but the masonry's integrity affects the whole structure's integrity. Whether it makes up the exterior walls, hearth, or chimney, or hidden underneath, if it has cracks in it, it can be the most dangerous part of the entire structure.

Foundations should be structurally strong, level, solid, firm, indestructible, and able to withstand both natural and unnatural disasters. Occasionally a crack may appear in a building's foundation. All cracks are not the same, some are more serious than others. However, all cracks in a structure's foundation need to be inspected and evaluated for any needed repairs. Repairs to the foundation of any structure are often expensive and could cause collateral damage to the building if not done properly. This is why the foundation you are building upon must be carefully inspected before building a structure. Any construction begins only after the foundation has been inspected and its integrity established.

An architect or master builder may have designed a beautiful home or addition with the perfect number of rooms in a layout that satisfies all the homeowner's requirements. You may have even selected the finest quality finishes, such as flooring, countertops, tiles for kitchen or baths, lighting, and the like. The interior design elements are important to most homeowners but not as important as the elements that "fortify" the home. We can look to insurance companies for insight into what those elements are. Before you are granted extended coverage of any kind, the insurance company performs what is called a "risk assessment" to determine your rates and coverage limits. Not surprisingly, that assessment does not place a lot of weight on the finishes and design elements of the home. Instead, they look at a home's location, the materials from which the house is built, things like impact resistant windows and doors, security elements (fire and burglary alarms), and the quality of the home's roof system. In some areas of the country, there are geographical and environmental considerations as well.

Believe it or not, exterior windows and doors help fortify a home. The function and style of the windows and the exterior doors (including garage doors) are very much a part of the overall design of any home. We rely on windows to bring in natural light and keep out the outside elements. When you have a house with a view or one with a more modern design, floor-to-ceiling windows are highly coveted. Other home styles have unique window and front door styles that go with their look. However, structural integrity, function, and form are more important than how they look.

In Florida, windows and doors are rated based on their ability to withstand storms such as hurricanes. Windows that are not made from quality materials or have not been installed properly can negatively impact a home's value. No one wants to live in a home with old, drafty windows that are not very energy efficient. They also don't want windows that can be easily compromised, as with burglary. People in Florida especially don't want windows or doors that can't withstand the winds and rain that are sure to come during the annual hurricane season. This is one reason why the installation of exterior windows and doors must follow strict building codes. Windows are needed to help us see the outside world, yet we also need them to provide protection against the outside world.

I have covered some of the major components of a house, but there is one part of the home that is extremely important, but, like masonry, is sometimes overlooked. I want to spend a little time talking about the roof system of a home. The roof is the structure that makes up the upper exterior covering of the building, and it is just as important as the foundation when it comes to the structural integrity of a home. It provides protection. All the contents underneath the roof are at risk of deterioration and destruction if the roof structure is not well constructed and properly fortified. The roof covers and protects a home from the elements, such as rain, snow, wind, and extreme temperatures. The building materials used in roof construction and their overall shape and form vary. Early roofs were often thatched or made from straw. However, today's modern construction materials include metal, asphalt shingles, slate, clay, or concrete tiles, and even stone-coated steel. The shape of the roof is also important. Flat, gable, hip, gambrel, A-frame, salt box, pitched, pyramid, and bonnet all describe roof style and form. The forms differences are determined by architectural style preferences and the function is based on geographical and environmental factors.

For example, structures subject to high snowfall are likely to have pitched or gable roofs instead of flat roofs so the snow and ice can slide off the structure more effectively. The materials, roof shape and style and how the roof is installed are all significant to how effective that roof will protect a home. This is why the roofing industry is strictly regulated. If the roof system fails, then the entire building structure below it will probably follow. The design, materials, and installation of roof systems must follow strict codes. If those codes are not followed, the building will likely not be eligible for insurance and will be at a higher risk of failure compared to those roof systems that are up to the latest building codes.

For new builds, the inside work continues after the foundation is laid and the framing work and roof are installed. Framing refers to installing floor joists, sub-floors, and the studs or boards that form the walls and roof trusses. The inside work for new construction includes things like electrical, plumbing, HVAC, insulation, and drywall installation. For major remodels any one of these may need to be touched. When you are creating your Dream Home, the inside work is just as important, if not more so, than the outside look of the home. Why? Because we experience our homes from the inside out.

When a realtor schedules a home tour for a prospective buyer, they don't start with the outside spaces. After the potential buyer gets a feel for the initial "curb appeal," the realtor will whisk the buyer(s) inside to look at the home's interior features and will spend most of their time showing those inside spaces. With that said, a lot of skilled resources are needed to complete the inside spaces of any home. They include electricians, plumbers, HVAC technicians, drywall specialists, tile installers, and flooring experts. In fact, electrical wiring, plumbing, and heating and cooling systems and ducts are essential elements that need licensed tradespeople to perform this work. The plumbing, electrical, and HVAC are like the arteriole vascular system of a home, and that is why it is very crucial to ensure that those areas are free from damage and have a good flow.

An *interior designer* may have been hired to ensure that the completed spaces meet the project's function, form, and style goals. They are usually brought on at the beginning of the project, especially for remodels, but can also be contracted later in the process to help ensure that the owner's style and preferences are implemented in the home. Interior designers are trained professionals with a working knowledge of textiles, materials, color, space planning, sustainability, health, safety, and building code requirements. In many cases, the homeowner fulfills the role of an interior designer. In all cases, this role helps to ensure that the overall look, function, and feel of a home is finished in ways that are exemplary. The finished product should match or exceed a homeowner's dreams for their home.

- 14 -

From Permits to Finished Product

In previous chapters, we explored some of the needful preparation associated with finding your dream home. Everything from carefully analyzing your experiences, to determining your "must haves," to setting your budget, and evaluating your options "wisely." We discovered that these steps not only apply to finding your physical dream home but also your dream relationship. The road to that dream relationship begins with two people, meeting and, after getting to know each other, agreeing to move forward together toward a permanent partnership where both parties can grow, advance goals, and gain gratifying life experiences. This permanent partnership or marriage is something that must be carefully constructed based on the preferences and requirements of the couple. Building a successful marriage is very similar to some of the other construction projects previously discussed. You must start with quality components, a solid foundation, and guidance from a master builder. Qualified experts and inspectors are also needed along the way.

Remember the permitting process I identified earlier? Let us now explore *permitting* from a relationship perspective. When my husband and I first met, he was in the final stages of a broken marriage and consequently dealing with a lot of brokenness. After a time, we ran into each other more frequently. I do not believe it was a coincidence. It was during those chance meetings and brief conversations that I got a glimpse of the type of man he was. I also learned that his interest in me in me was growing. After this realization, I knew I had to quickly decide whether to allow things to continue or to *nip it in the bud,* as was my custom. In a sense, I had to decide whether to issue him a *permit.* Because of his most recent relationship status and not being entirely sure what his intentions were, I made the initial decision to let him know he did *not* have my permission to proceed. There were some obvious and other not so obvious reasons for my decision. The truth of the matter was that he was just not available or in any position to add me or any other relationship to his already complicated life.

> In a sense, I had to decide whether to issue him a *permit.*

One important lesson I learned early in life is this: *I am the one in authority concerning who I allow into my life, and I must be very careful about who I give that authority to.* I do not remember exactly when I learned this. Probably knowledge I gained over time through the process observation. It was through the lens of a daughter watching her mother and other women having to make similar decisions and then watching their outcomes play out. What I learned was this: *It doesn't matter what someone does to impress you or how adept they may be in the art of wooing you, or how skilled in manipulation they are, or how sorry you may feel for them in their circumstances. We all have in our possession the power and authority to grant or reject every attempt to gain access to us.* That kind of power should never be abused, and my job is to make sure of it. So, with that said, when I issue a relationship *permit*, I must also be able to clearly communicate my unique expectations and what is needed to fulfill my permit requirements. Next, I must then take special care to inspect the works of the person I issued the permit to. Why? Because just like with building permits, my current and future safety is at stake!

I know both women and men who issued *permits* to the wrong people. They hooked up with people who looked and sounded sturdy and established, but were found out to be *faulty fabrications* that did not hold up well under pressure. You are in big trouble when words like "shoddy" and "unstable," terms usually reserved for structures, are best used to describe your mate. I, too, have dated a *faulty fabrication*. I think most people have or will at some point find themselves in this predicament. I believe it comes with the territory when dating. The bottom line is that issuing *permits* to people who do not have the qualifications, capability, or the know-how is always risky business. The potential for future happiness and success seems great in the beginning, but if they do not pass a proper inspection, then all progress should be immediately halted. In both the construction world and in relationships, this is called a "red flag."

The *red flag* is used as a universal warning system, and it is a signal to *stop* because of potential danger. I believe that *red flags* appear throughout our life experiences but are often missed. Especially when we are excited and in too much of a hurry to get to a specific desired outcome. That is when we are most likely to take shortcuts, fail to do our due diligence, and ignore the standards that were previously set. Proper *vetting* helps us to choose wisely and build precisely. *Vetting* is defined as *the act or process of appraising or checking a person or thing for suitability, accuracy, or validity*. Anyone that you entrust to build something should be properly vetted. There is too much at stake, not too. Only after proper vetting should you proceed with permits. For marriage, the permit and vetting process help to predict the structural integrity of the couple and the validity of their plans. When a couple decides they want to take on the ultimate project of building a life together through marriage, it is assumed that the framework of *commitment* has already been established. There is a myth that in getting married you are guaranteeing commitment. Marriage does not produce commitment, but rather it symbolizes the presumed commitment a couple already has. Marriage is when the actual commitment of a couple is celebrated in a ceremonial way.

Commitment represents the framework of all well-built marriages. Just as the foundation and framing work are some of the first areas that are scrutinized when permits are given for new buildings, the same holds true with marriage. If commitment is the framework, then love (the enduring and self-sacrificing kind) is the foundation. Falling in love kicks off the entire project. In a perfect world, people meet, fall in love, make commitments to one another and then make plans to build a happy life together. Of course, we know it is not as simple as those Hollywood romantic comedies suggest. Do not get me wrong, it can happen in precisely that way. There are other times, however, when we may find ourselves in love with someone who is not equally in love with us. Sometimes we get hooked up with people who are more in love with what comes with us, things like position, prestige, and many other privileges that come with our love. Red flag!

Although love is universal, its meaning may differ from person to person. People of faith understand love in a particular way. Christians, for example, see *love* as the motive, measurement, and the manner of their faith. **Motive**: "For God so *loved* the world that He gave His only begotten son that whoever believes in him should not perish but have eternal life" John 3:16 (NIV). **Measurement:** "Greater *love* has no one than this, that someone lay down his life for his friends" John 15:13 (NIV). **Manner:** "*Love* is patient and kind. *Love* is not jealous or boastful or proud or rude. It does not demand its own way. It is not irritable, and it keeps no record of being wronged. It does not rejoice about injustice but rejoices whenever the truth wins out. Love never gives up, never loses faith, is always hopeful, and endures through every circumstance." 1 Corinthians 13:4-7 (NLT). This manner makes all the difference. Other faiths have similar interpretations.

Remember that *structural integrity* refers to the ability of something to hold together under the stress of a heavy load. Bridges, buildings, statues, monuments are all things that must have structural integrity. Likewise, my husband and I, as a couple, must also have structural integrity. Sometimes, as people, we discover parts of us that are weakened, fractured, or unsteady from our experiences. In a sense, those things must also be torn down, removed, replaced, or reestablished so that our relationships can stand under pressure. So, what are some examples of things that may need to be torn down or demolished in a relationship that could jeopardize its structural integrity? Some examples may include unresolved past trauma or abuse, addictions, conflicting sexual orientations or desires, opposite belief systems, toxic support systems, mental or emotional illness, and even spiritual depravity or decay. Any of these can contribute to a relationship's failure.

> My husband and I, as a couple, must also have structural integrity.

The rule of thumb is this: if it cannot be properly repaired then it should be replaced, especially if it impacts the foundation or core structure of the thing. If these issues are identified but not properly addressed, then the relationship will gradually and progressively decline and possibly fall into a state of disrepair. Relationships, just like buildings with structural integrity issues, may eventually be condemned or flagged as "unfit for occupancy." Demolition and repair actions are essential for addressing issues that affect the structural integrity of any relationship. This includes habits, behaviors, toxic relationships, and even beliefs.

Not that we are to "demolish" or destroy any actual persons who jeopardize the relationship. However, the context of some of those relationships may need to be broken down and reestablished. When I say context, I am referring to those unspoken rules of engagement that come from prior personal history. For example, there are parents who are very involved in their children's lives, even throughout adulthood.

They do not recognize or respect boundaries. There are very few areas of their adult children's lives that they feel they should not have access to. These are the parents who failed to adjust their parental role as their kids developed and matured. Parenting a seven-year-old is very different from parenting a twenty-seven-year-old. Some parents cannot let go of their control, and they remain enmeshed in every aspect of their children's lives in ways that are sometimes not very healthy for either party.

When those adult children marry, the parent may not be so willing to step back to transition into a new or different role in their lives. When that happens, the adult child should not demolish the relationship with that parent, but they should work toward repairing it. Unhealthy or damaged relationships between parents and their adult children require the type of careful reconstruction that is reserved for historic buildings or precious works of art. Repairing cherished things, including relationships that are worn and damaged over time by different conditions and circumstances, is slow and meticulous work. It requires patience. This work sometimes requires help from a restoration specialist. With damaged relationships, a restoration specialist may include a well-respected family member or friend of the family, therapists, counselors, or clergy.

Relationships, particularly marriage, need windows too. Why? Because everyone needs light (insight, truth, wisdom, positive regard) to survive. What relationship can survive without visible light? To some, this may sound superstitious, but I believe that there are forces lurking about us (some call it evil), threatening to destroy us by using jealousy, envy, temptation, negativity, and sometimes even family and friends to do it. How a couple sees the outside world determines how much light they prefer. All couples need to evaluate their "windows". Windows here refers to how a couple sees the world, their marriage, and each other and how much truth, wisdom, or positive regard they allow to shine through.

Regulation and codes, I believe, also apply to couples. My husband and I follow strict codes of conduct that cover our marriage. We defined them early in our relationship, both formally and informally. Like building codes or a code of ethics, I will refer to these rules as a couple's *code of covering*. For my husband and I, one of our codes is that *we choose our words carefully and always speak respectfully toward each other*, even when we are angry or disappointed about something the other one said or did. Another one of our codes is that *if one of us feels hurt or disrespected or if we feel that the other person may have been hurt by something we said or did, we have agreed to address it, to call it out and talk it out as soon as possible.* We will also allow for a reasonable cooling-off period if tempers are too high to immediately talk it through. Following this rule means that neither of us must sacrifice our feelings for the sake of the other. My feelings are not more important than my husband's or vice versa. Both of our feelings matter, and they should matter a lot to both of us.

We also decided long ago that our marriage — and marriage itself — is much bigger than the two of us. We both believe that *marriage is a sacred and holy sacrament and a lifelong covenant between the bride and groom.* We also believe that we were called to this in the same way that clergy are called into ministry. I say this because, according to the scriptures, we find that the relationship between Jesus Christ and the church is patterned after marriage. That means in accordance with our faith, when we said, "I do," it meant that we entered a lifetime contractual partnership with God and each other. This covenant was not just for our sake, but also for the sake of our family, our community, our family, humanity, and God's Kingdom. I know that sounds like a serious and heavy commitment to make, because it is.

Unfortunately, not all couples, not even all Christian couples, fully consider this before they marry. From the very beginning, my husband and I have been mindful that our behavior (how we nurture and protect each other) is based on the premise that our marriage is much bigger than us. Just as the building codes ensure that the roof protects the structure from wind, rain, and extreme temperatures, relationships must follow codes that offer protection against destructive forces as well. For people of faith, their religion's sacred texts are always a good source to understand conduct. Note the helpful scriptures included in this book. Non-believers should explore this by talking to their partner about every mutual expectation they can think of. An important topic for all couples is how to engage with each other in times of agreement and conflict. Some sort of premarital counseling is highly recommended for establishing these things early. For those who are already married, it is never too late to establish ground rules in your relationship. Those ground rules form a *roof* over your relationship.

When it comes to building a marriage, a lot of inside work is required. Healthy marriages are based on love and commitment (foundation and framing), effective communication channels (wiring, plumbing, and HVAC), and a plan that best fits the goals of the individuals which consider their preferences, functional and safety needs (interior design). In construction, the framing comprises fitting materials together to give the building its structure, support, and shape. In relationships, that is exactly what commitment does. It is the material that provides the structure, support, and shape for all healthy relationships. Without the framing, you have no structure. You would have a foundation slab with no hope of a building ever taking shape. No walls, floors, roofs, windows, doors, none of these things can be installed without framing. None of the wonderful benefits of marriage can be realized without the framework of commitment set on a foundation of love.

The other lifeline in a healthy marriage is communication. Using our construction theme, you can compare communication channels to the wiring, plumbing, and HVAC channels of the home. Think about the condition of any home that has faulty electrical wiring, bad plumbing, and inefficient, poorly installed duct work. It does not matter how beautiful the home is on the inside, or how amazing the curb appeal is from the outside, if those elements aren't working

> None of the wonderful benefits of marriage can be realized without the framework of commitment set on a foundation of love.

properly, the whole house could be deemed uninhabitable. If you have encountered a couple with communication problems, the same term (uninhabitable) comes to mind. This is a good segue to talk about why inspections are so important. Just like the risks associated with buying a home that has not been thoroughly inspected, the same can be said about entering marriage without inspection. Premarital counseling is an example of an inspection process that helps couples determine the relationships' structural integrity and to get guidance on how to best keep it together. Counseling is the best place to uncover these things. If inspections are required in home construction, how much more important are they in marriage? Getting married with no premarital counseling is like buying a home that is "as-is" with no inspection contingency.

As you may have noticed, I have been writing this commentary from my perspective as a Christian woman. I wish I could say that Christian couples achieve better outcomes in marriage than non-Christian ones, but that is just not the case. Christian marriages fail at the same rate as non-Christian ones. Being a follower of Christ does not make you immune to all the pitfalls and challenges of marriage in these modern times. I say modern times because, as technology changes, so do the societal norms that drive our behaviors. Think about social media as an example. Social media is defined as *interactive technologies that facilitate the creation and sharing of information, ideas, interests, and other forms of expression through virtual communities and networks.* Popular platforms such as Facebook, Instagram, Twitter/X, TikTok, and Snapchat fall under this umbrella. Not surprisingly, recent studies have shown that social media usage directly impacts social behavior. This can happen organically (naturally with no extra help) and other times it is carefully engineered to move people from one opinion to another, one ideology to another, and one set of values to another. It is also used to drive spending habits in very intentional ways. This form of technology can have both positive and negative effects. On a positive note, social media is useful in helping people feel more connected to their family, friends, and the outside world. It can share information, and for creatives to share their art, to a wide audience in real time.

However, social media usage can be a very slippery slope, especially for couples. I think those apps should come with warning labels that describe their harmful effects. According to a study published in *Computers in Human Behavior*, a link was identified between social media usage and decreased marriage quality and satisfaction. The study results predicts that people who rarely engage with social media are 11% happier in their marriages than people who do. According to the study, higher levels of social media are linked to marital problems such as infidelity, an increase in conflicts, jealousy, with some even leading to divorce. Technology continues to advance with each generation. Artificial Intelligence is the current phase of technological advancement that will radically change how things are built as well as our societal norms.

Each set of tools that are created by and used by humanity improve our quality of life. However, a wise person once said, *"A fool with a tool is still a fool!"* One tenant of Christianity is found in a popular Bible verse, John 3:16, which begins with these words…. "For God so loved the world, that He gave…." This one tiny verse answers the who, what, why, and how questions about our faith and serves as a universal model verse for marriage. All couples can make this scripture personal by rewording it in this way: "*Because we love* each other, *we give* of ourselves to one other, just as God did for us, and if we believe in this love and behave accordingly, then our marriage shall never die but instead it will live and thrive for the rest of our lives."

Building a successful marriage is difficult and complex construction work, regardless of a person's faith or traditions. Everyone needs some sort of blueprint or set of instructions to follow to increase their chances of building something sound that will withstand the many tests of time. I have found that following Christ's example in both theory and practice has given me the best pathway to building my dream relationship. Christ was a carpenter by trade. His teachings have been a firm foundation for me and many others in our relationships.

Big Reveal#7

For a new build, major reno, or marriage, make sure that the proper authorizations have been secured, proper codes are followed, and inspections conducted to ensure that you have a solid foundation so that whatever you are building will be able to carry the load that comes with it.

Helpful Scriptures

"And He is before all things, and in him all things hold together."
Colossians 1:17 (ESV)

"For we are Gods fellow workers. You are Gods field, Gods building. According to the grace of God given to me, like a skilled master builder I laid a foundation, and someone else is building upon it. Let each one take care how he builds upon it. For no one can lay a foundation other than that which is laid, which is Jesus Christ. Now if anyone builds on the foundation with gold, silver, precious stones, wood, hay, straw — each one's work will become manifest, for the Day will disclose it, because it will be revealed by fire, and the fire will test what sort of work each one has done."
1 Corinthians 3:9-15 (ESV)

- 15 -

The Big Reveal

The process of building or rebuilding any structure or part of an existing structure is filled with its share of challenges. Even projects with the best, most highly credentialed builders, architects, general contractors, project managers, interior designers, and skilled laborers can run into problems. With persistence, however, the day will finally come when the vision is realized, and all the hard work and effort can finally be revealed to those who have been eagerly waiting. The *Big Reveal* is finally here!

First, I want to explore this notion of a *reveal*. If you have not guessed it, I watch a lot of home improvement shows. In fact, the only reality-based television shows that I consistently enjoy watching are those that have anything to do with real estate. It does not matter if it is about houses, resorts, houseboats, RVs, tiny homes, cabins, huts, and everything in between. Whether the show is based on a couple hunting for their next home, home away from home, house on wheels, on the water, expensive zip codes, or inexpensive ones, these shows all have one thing in common. As camera crews follow potential buyers or homeowners along their journey, with all the plot twists and turns that are signature to these types of shows, the ending or last segment of the show is always the same, and it is referred to as the *reveal*. If you get hooked during the show's first segment, you will most likely hang in there for the reveal. Even if you are a notorious channel surfer changing the channel at every commercial break (like my husband), you will, in most cases find your way back to catch the end or the *Big Reveal*. Why? Because you need closure, or at least that is what I tell myself. Sometimes, I will have a few things going on while one of those shows is playing in the background, but then, without fail, I will stop everything to pay careful attention to what happens at the end. Did they choose the condo in the city center or the single-family home in the burbs, was it the cabin by the lake, mountainside retreat, Malibu mansion, Lower East Side loft, luxury "Class A" motor home, "Fifth Wheel" travel trailer, or some other unexpected option? Did the owners decide to love it or list it? After all the budget shortfalls and last-minute changes, how did the remodel turn out?

The *reveal* is when we see the result of all that effort. The word *reveal* simply means *to make known*. The reveal gives those of us watching a glimpse at what the owners will go through to achieve their heart's desire. Along the way, we get to see small snapshots of the personalities of the people involved in the overall process, and, based on what we saw, we try to guess the ending. That, by far, is the best part. I could watch these storylines play out every day, but it is a television show with the sole purpose of entertaining us.

In real life, new builds and remodel projects also have a *reveal* that happens at the end. It describes the point when you walk through the home and focus on the project's finished work. It is the moment everyone has been waiting for. It may not be as dramatic as the TV version, but it should be as exciting for you, if not more so. You get to see the results of the investment of time, money, creativity, vision, craftsmanship, and ingenuity. I will never forget that feeling of satisfaction and joy after the completion of a remodel of the kitchen and bathrooms in our previous home. After living in a construction "dust" zone for over six weeks, preparing meals in our outside kitchen with large sheets of thick plastic serving as makeshift walls and floor coverings, the *reveal* could not come soon enough. While drywall, tile, plumbing fixtures, cabinetry, appliances, and countertops were being installed, I, of course, took several sneak peaks before the last inspection. Even with my advanced inspections, nothing compared to the last walk-through with our designer. The moment we walked through to

> You get to see the results of the investment of time, money, creativity, vision, craftsmanship, and ingenuity.

see what the "after" looked like was a special one. The pleasure was not just ours, it was shared with everyone who took part in the project, and with others who simply waited patiently to see it come to fruition. Neighbors and friends helped us relive that joy with each subsequent *reveal*.

- 16 -

The Big Reveal

The *reveal* of your dream home marks the occasion when the final realization of your dreams is made known to you and other observers. Such as the case when a couple finds lasting love and builds a healthy, committed and satisfying life together. There are probably lots of *mini reveals* that happen along the way. To experience the awe and majesty of a *big reveal*, you must take notice of what the "before" looked like so you can fully appreciate the transformation. Some say that a couple's wedding day represents their *big reveal*. I disagree. The real *reveal* happens around six or seven years after the wedding. It is only after a couple has lived through the type of deconstruction and reconstruction that only happens during *the struggle* of joining two very different people together. The *struggle* refers to the time and effort applied in making a commitment and living it. Everything that happens before that mark is merely the hope of what the couple sets out to achieve. The plot twists and turns that we see in those half-hour home improvement shows are not far off in the telling.

Much like those shows, most couples start with an idea of what their "happily ever after" looks like and, just like those shows, their vision usually costs way more than they had ever budgeted or planned for. Unfortunately, many couples don't take the serious time and thought required to count up the costs ahead of time. Marriage costs. It costs both parties something. To achieve a successful, soul-quenching, and otherwise satisfying relationship, both individuals must love in very self-sacrificing ways. You cannot have one person who is 100% "self-sacrificing," meaning they make all decisions based on what is best for their partner and for the relationship first, and the other partner who is the exact opposite (self-serving). It may sound like a good match, self-sacrificing and self-serving, but that pairing never holds up.

In my marriage, my husband and I work together under this notion: *the success and well-being of my partner and our marriage are my priority, and any sacrifice I make toward both is worth it*. My partner is worth it! Your marriage is worth it! At some point, you both must be convinced of this. Although it is true that some of the best things in life are free, a successful marriage comes at a cost. It requires an investment of personal time, energy, attention, finances, mental focus, and emotional intelligence, to name a few. However, it goes beyond investing in those things. We must also *divest* of some other things when we enter marriage. Things like our pride, ego, and our self-centered ambitions. Sometimes certain relationships may suffer and change dramatically because of your marriage, but you both must have the resolve that your marriage is worth it.

The reason both parties must agree that the changes and sacrifices that come with marriage are worth it is because at different times you and your partner may find yourselves frustrated, confused, or afraid during the struggle and may forget the joy-filled commitment you made to each other at the beginning. When doubt creeps in (and it will), or when conflicts seem impossible to resolve, you can encourage yourselves that whatever you must do to get through to the other side of it for your marriage's sake is worth it. So no, the *big reveal* does not happen on your wedding day. It happens after a few iterations of unexpected problems, budget shortfalls, skillful demolition, and rebuilding that a couple can truly celebrate their *big reveal*. You probably will not have a camera and production crew there, but it will be no less spectacular of an event. I encourage couples to do a virtual walk-through with each other, remembering everything you went through, and with joy and excitement, celebrate your accomplishments. Couples can do this during an anniversary celebration, or a quiet day of reflection. You can even include those who took part in your marriage success, like family, friends, and trusted advisors.

For every anniversary, my husband and I swap stories of our entire relationship timeline. We reminisce about our courtship, our early years of marriage, the highs and lows of every part and we end up sharing our gratitude for how far we have come. This is a time for counting our blessings and, more importantly, a time for looking forward and imagining what the future still holds for us. Each year we are together, we are more convinced that our best days are ahead of us. Our *big reveal* happens every time we reflect upon and report the success of our marriage.

Big Reveal #8

The big reveal for your dream home is to show off the finished work of your creation. The big reveal for your marriage is to show off God's handiwork of enduring love and faithful commitment through us.

Helpful Scriptures

"For we are his workmanship, created in Christ Jesus for good works, which God prepared beforehand, that we should walk in them."
Ephesians 2:10 (ESV)

"For you created my inmost being you knit me together in my mother's womb. I praise you because I am fearfully and wonderfully made; your works are wonderful, I know that full well."
Psalms 139-13-14 (NIV)

- 17 -

Pride of Ownership

A good measure of how much you treasure something can be seen in your *pride of ownership*. What do I mean by *pride of ownership*? First, *it refers to a feeling of obligation, stewardship, and devotion to the things of value that one owns*. This involves performing routine maintenance of their property inside and out, as well as making periodic investments in property upgrades. Secondly, *pride of ownership* is demonstrated by how a person describes the thing of value they are most proud of. For example, if someone were to ask me to describe my home, it would sound something like this: "I absolutely love my home. My husband and I consider it our dream home. It is everything we desire, and every square foot of it helps make us feel happy and at peace, and I know it is the place our family was meant to be." We have *pride of ownership*, as evidenced by what we do and what we say about our home.

Our home resides in a community of townhouses that are divided into four phases that we call *villages*. The term *villages* make our community sound very quaint. I was told that the term was chosen to describe each section of homes as they were completed. The first phase of development consisted of a certain number of homes and buildings, approximately four to five townhomes per building, depending on the size of each one. There are two-unit sizes, the two-bedroom or the three-bedroom option. After the first phase was completed, the builder continued to the next phase, which included several more buildings with four to five homes in each one. This continued along a small peninsula along the intercostal, giving most units a water view. In total, there are four phases of development. The term *phases* does not sound very inviting, which is why I am sure someone cleverly decided to use the term *villages* instead. The truth is the term is the perfect description for our community.

As homeowners in my current neighborhood, we are proud of our homes, and as neighbors, we are proud of the phase or village we live in. At the same time, we feel deeply connected to the greater community. Friendliness is the rule and not the exception. Neighbors are intentional about getting to know each other and displaying a sincere regard for one another. There is a digital community newsletter that keeps us all connected. New homeowners are featured in it with a front-page story describing who they are, where they came from, and what drew them to our slice of paradise. Because we are a waterfront community, the newsletter also contains tips from a resident boat captain about current conditions for fishing near or offshore and recommendations for scenic recreational cruises. Reviews of local restaurants and points of interest are often highlighted as well. There is nothing overly unique about a neighborhood newsletter, but it is one small part of what makes living here special.

My husband and I are what I would describe as "folksy." We have a reputation for sharing our home with friends and family for food and fellowship. Since we have been together, we have met many dear friends who started as neighbors. Some would describe us as your typical *southern socializers*. Not to be confused with the term *socialite*, which is a completely different vibe. Before deciding on our current home, we looked at one unit that was for sale a few doors down within the same phase or village. On the day of our viewing appointment with our realtor, we were greeted by two little girls, sisters aged ten and eight. They lived next door to the unit we were scheduled to view. As we got out of the car to look around while waiting for our realtor, the girls approached us with big smiles, eagerly asking us if we were going to be their new neighbors. We smiled but tried not to act overly familiar with them, remembering what we taught our own daughter about "stranger danger." I believe I responded with "we are not sure yet", all the while thinking to myself, "what perfect little ambassadors!" It meant a lot because our daughter, who was not with us, was around the same age. Although we did not purchase the unit next door to them, the girls and our daughter became fast friends. That was the first of many signs that confirmed we had been led to the right location.

From that moment until now, I have been amazed at the number of "folksy" people that are here from all over the country who have settled in this seaside village we call home. Days after we moved in, one of our neighbors from the adjacent phase/village came by to introduce herself and to give me a copy of the resident directory. She asked me if I would like our contact information to be included in the newest edition, as the association management company had already provided her with our names. I found her to be a kindred spirit with kind eyes and an undeniable love for people. Since living here, we have met different people from all walks of life, both permanent and seasonal residents.

To some of our friendliest neighbors, walking, sitting or fishing at the community dock, taking out the trash, or even washing our cars in the driveway seem to serve as "invitations" to chat. Conversations are always interesting, sometimes brief, and mostly cordial as we try to adhere to the unwritten rule of avoiding conversations about politics and religion. Ironically, many of our neighbors have come to know that my husband is a Baptist preacher, even though he rarely mentions it. I think it comes out naturally when he talks to people. It's hard for him not to talk about the goodness of God, and folks see us leaving for church most Sundays. One of the neighbors always respectfully refers to him "as Pastor Bo" while others just call him "Bo." I find it endearing. Of course, I would be remiss if I failed to mention that there were some neighbors who did not initially share warmth and "friendly neighbor" vibe. I don't know if we were the first, but when we moved in, we were the only African American family living here. Don't get me wrong, I saw other blacks visiting. My guess was that some of those visitors may have been part of a blended family or were here visiting a friend or co-worker. We were an all-black family living in an all-white subdivision on the Gulf Coast of Florida. With that reality, the odds were very high that we would run into some people, who were not exactly happy to see us move in. We laugh about it now.

My husband experienced more than one confrontation with men in our community who questioned him about who he was, where he lived, and whether he had a right to be here. In another time and place, he probably would have been asked to show his "papers." But, instead of meeting their rudeness with anger and bitterness, using godly wisdom, my husband boldly introduced himself to them as their newest neighbor with a healthy dose of southern charm, confidence, and Christian courtesy. He slowly but surely won them all over by waving, smiling, and warmly speaking to those with the chilliest dispositions. This was easy for him because that is simply who he is. Besides, those few unpleasant encounters were outnumbered by the majority of people, who made it a point to get to know us and who made us feel welcome through their open expressions of friendliness and kind regard towards each of us.

As I write this, a few more black families have moved into our subdivision, adding more *pepper* to our little melting pot by the sea. I am grateful that happiness fills our home, so we make it a point to allow some of it to spill out with us whenever we come or go. Taking a stroll down to the beach and back, playing catch in our front driveway, or walking to one of the community pools are all times when our joy and pride of ownership go with us. It is not the "I am better than you" kind of pride, but the "I am grateful to be here" kind. It is in that spirit of gratitude that takes great care of our home. We proudly perform routine cleaning inside and out and ensure that proactive maintenance is performed as needed. We also have installed upgrades such as awnings, new appliances, and replacement windows to enhance our home's value.

An appraiser recently came to prepare an assessment of the market value of our home. He explicitly said to me that our home showed a great deal of *"pride of ownership"*. He compared ours to other homes he had recently appraised that were in similar locations, but he noted that some of them reflected a *lack of investment in the needful things*. This appraiser gave us the highest compliment you can give a homeowner. He affirmed that great care was being taken in maintaining our home, as reflected by both its aesthetic look and overall condition.

> It is in that spirit of gratitude that takes great care of our home.

For anyone buying, building, or rebuilding their dream home, a crucial step is to identify the things you must do to maintain the appearance and functionality of your investment. Certain design elements of your home may become a maintenance priority. For example, if flooring is a key feature, then regular cleaning or polishing should be scheduled using the appropriate products and techniques. Ceramic tile, wood, carpet, area rugs, vinyl plank, concrete, or marble require specific cleaning and maintenance protocols. Sometimes you may need to hire someone to perform scheduled maintenance or purchase specific tools and products so you can do it yourself. If not, over time, your prized decor elements will become a dirty, dull, full-blown disaster. Likewise, things like windows and doors, lighting, appliances, plumbing fixtures, and more require periodic attention. Time and regular use lead to deterioration if you are not intentional about combating the natural effects of wear and tear. It does not matter how much you initially paid or how much time and effort you put into the initial placement or installation of the décor in question, it is all about the upkeep. Upkeep refers to our actions to help maintain the quality and longevity of our homes. We do this by focusing on preserving, repairing and sometimes replacing the unrepairable. Homeowners should try to always be about the business of preservation and repair. Let us first look at what preservation means.

My internet dictionary describes *preservation* as: *(a) the act or process of keeping something in existence; and (b) the act or process of keeping something safe from damage or deterioration.* Since we probably do not actively work toward preserving things we do not treasure or love, the unspoken but clearly most essential part of preservation is love. Now, let us look at what *repair* means. It is an action verb. It means to *(a) restore to a good or sound condition after decay or damage; and (b) to restore or renew by any process of making good or strengthening. Repairing* can be part of *the preservation* process. Routine cleaning and proactive maintenance are also part of the *preservation* process. Remember, we *do not preserve what we do not treasure and love.* I coined this phrase for a reason that connects back to my faith. Take note that throughout the Bible there are many examples of God *preserving* the godly, meaning taking care of, restoring, and delivering those who placed their faith and trust in Him. God set the ultimate example by *preserving* those He loved the most. People of faith and nonbelievers alike can follow this example in their homes, in their marriages, and in their overall lives. We all should take great care of the things we treasure and love.

- 18 -

Pride of Ownership

When people look at me and my husband and, more specifically, at our marriage, I hope they see what the appraiser saw in our home: a genuine *pride of ownership*. Now that may sound a little strange when describing a married couple. We don't own each other, and one should never consider their spouse as their possession. "God don't mean people to own people" was that poignant line in the movie "Harriet" that immediately comes to mind. So, I do not own my husband, and he does not own me. We have, however, taken ownership or rather responsibility for this committed relationship we are in, called marriage. Our marriage, like our home, requires regular maintenance and investment in the needful things.

When thinking about pride of ownership in our marriage, my recent experience with the appraiser stands out. When he first walked into our home, he began making comparisons to other homes that were

> Our marriage, like our home, requires regular maintenance and investment in the needful things.

similar in size and location. He remarked on key differences that stood out to him. From the floor to the ceiling, he frequently smiled while taking measurements and jotting down notes about his observations. He asked questions about recent upgrades and remarked favorably on how beautiful and peaceful our home appeared. This surprised me because we didn't have time to have our home professionally cleaned before he arrived, and I did nothing in terms of staging to help shape his first impressions. Essentially, what he rolled up on that day was what he got. I was happy that he could look beyond the clutter on my desk and my daughter's craft table, and several other areas that were clean, but not exactly tidy, and could identify beauty, peace, and great value.

When people meet my husband and I, like the appraiser, they also make hidden assessments regarding the condition of our marriage and perhaps even the relative value of it. It is human nature for people to make comparisons to other marriages they have seen, including their own. We hope that when they look at us and make comparisons, they also find beauty, peace, and great value like the appraiser did. The beauty of our mutual love and respect for one another, the peace that comes with being in one accord with God and with each other, and the value that our marriage adds to our family, our community, and beyond. This is our goal, to demonstrate proper *pride of ownership* for our marriage.

Big Reveal #9

*After your dreams have been realized,
be in a constant pattern of preserving,
repairing, and restoring what was built.*

Helpful Scriptures

"My people will live in peaceful dwelling places, in
secure homes, in undisturbed places of rest,"
Isaiah 32:18. (NIV)

"Love the Lord, all his faithful people! The Lord
preserves those who are true to him,"
Psalm 31:23 (NIV)

- 19 -

Gratitude

When observing excellent results of hard labor, creativity, and ingenuity, the best response one can give is "Thank you." In fact, it is my opinion that "Thank you" is an appropriate beginning and ending to any event, project, or endeavor. Although there are tons of scriptures about giving thanks, it is obviously not a practice that is exclusive to people of faith. When a meal is good, when the work was done right, when your expectations were met or exceeded, "Thank you" is one of a few appropriate responses that is universally accepted in any country in any language. When I host a meal, facilitate a workshop, or lead a meeting, it is my practice to thank the participants twice, once at the beginning of the event and again at the very end. I don't remember anyone ever telling me to do this. It is a habit I picked up over my years of experience. A carefully timed "Welcome, good seeing you, thanks for coming" is usually my opener, and "I enjoyed our time together, thanks again for coming" is my closer. Why twice? Why thank anyone at all? For some, it is simply a matter of good manners. For me, that is certainly part of it, but the greater part has more to do with what happens when I express gratitude versus the times when I do not.

The effects of gratitude are enormous, although often underrated. I remember reading something recently that confirmed what I had suspected. Essentially, whatever I was reading suggested that expressing gratitude improves physical and mental health, strengthens social relationships, produces positive emotional states, and helps us cope with stressful times in our lives. It is remarkable to me how this small two-word phrase (thank you) can create such an enormous impact. I also learned that researchers have recently discovered that expressing gratitude increases certain neurochemicals in the brain and body. The body gets a surge of pleasure-inducing hormones like dopamine, serotonin, and oxytocin. These produce feelings of closeness, connection, and happiness. As a result, people who maintain an attitude of gratitude are happier, live longer, and have better health outcomes. Who knew that being thankful could do all that? Ironically, those are the same feelings we want to experience in our homes. Therefore, I believe it is so important to take the time to be intentional about giving thanks, especially for all the work that went into creating your dream home. Thank your banker, realtor, builder, general contractor, architect, interior designer, sub-contractors, and any and everybody who played a part in making your dreams come true. Of course, it is always a good idea to thank your mate for the part they played in the process as well. People of faith should always thank the Creator God as well.

> It is remarkable to me how this small two-word phrase (thank you) can create such an enormous impact.

Gratitude should not be merely a closing afterthought. It is a beneficial part of the building process itself. In fact, I liken gratitude to an invisible building material that helps to build up and encourage all those involved in your project. Think about it, how many people help an *ungrateful* person? Not many. How many people go out of their way to help someone who appreciates their work and has a grateful attitude? It is no coincidence that I am wrapping things up with a chapter about gratitude. I happen to be writing this final chapter near the Thanksgiving holiday here in the US. Everything I read, see online, or on TV commercials reminds me of how important it is to give thanks. This time of year, reminds me of those childhood art projects made from fall colored construction paper and white school glue that depicted one or more elements from our country's Thanksgiving tradition. We made turkeys using everything from colored paper to paint and sometimes food items such as pasta noodles or beans.

Those pilgrim hats were my favorite. I remember being in plays acting out the scene from what we were told was our country's first Thanksgiving. However, years later I learned the true story of what happened at Plymouth, Massachusetts, in 1621. It was not exactly the scene our history books described. A more accurate depiction of a traditional "Thanksgiving" celebration in the Americas is believed to have happened when a Spanish explorer named Pedro Menendez de Avile invited members of the Timucua tribe for a meal after holding a mass to thank God for the explorer and his crew's safe arrival to what is now St. Augustine, Florida in 1565. There are other accounts that British explorers may have commemorated a day of Thanksgiving to God in December 1619, when they arrived safely at the banks of the James River in Virginia. Across the border to our north, Canada was holding their own Thanksgiving celebration as early as 1578 to commemorate a successful expedition and to give thanks for the safety of those involved. So, the practice did not begin in this country with the Pilgrims, contrary to commonly accepted belief.

It does not matter who we attribute the first Thanksgiving celebration in this country to. What I know as a believer is that gratitude pleases God. According to the scriptures, as the story goes, when Moses led his people out of Egypt and were stopped by what they thought was an unsurmountable obstacle, the Red Sea, God intervened and parted the sea so they could escape. On the other side of the sea, the people looked back and watched their enemies drown when God let the sea return to its original state. Before Moses and the people continued in their great escape, they stopped and gave thanks. In fact, the entire book of Exodus 15 is dedicated to giving thanks for that awesome miracle at the Red Sea. So, we now know that gratitude not only makes us feel better, but it also pleases God. When we say, "Thank you" to those who took part in some work or effort that we are involved in, we should remember to thank God for orchestrating it. When you have obtained your dream house or your dream marriage and consider everything it took to get there, express your gratitude, just like Moses and the early explorers in the US and Canada. In some cases, a ceremonial act of gratitude is warranted. I believe that expressing gratitude is as important to the building process as getting permits. You can certainly build a house or a marriage without saying thank you, but the true value of your investment will never fully be recognized if you do not. *If you treasure it, be thankful for it!*

Here we are, at the end of my *big reveal*. This journey began with me describing what most people dream about obtaining within their lifetimes. We explored the source of our wants, needs, and must haves. We learned about counting up the cost of what we desire, choosing wisely, and contingencies. We talked about the work of a trusted "Master Builder," and that special permission (or permits) must be issued before building. We also learned that demolition (tearing down to make room for the new) was also sometimes part of the process. We spent more time focusing on the building process, from laying the proper foundation to inside work and adding finishing touches based on our preferences and desires. After sharing personal insights about the different building stages and how to best make our dreams a reality, we learned about the importance of preservation, repair, and maintenance in relation to *pride of ownership*. Finally, we learned the importance of expressing gratitude at the beginning, end, and throughout our journey. Most importantly, I hope that every reader is able to see how each of these steps can apply to both building your dream home and your dream marriage. Thank you for reading!

> *If you treasure it,
> be thankful for it!*

Big Reveal#10

Gratitude means having a grateful attitude that inspires others and affirms our appreciation for everything and everybody that we love, value and treasure most, especially our homes and marriages.

Helpful Scriptures

"You will be enriched in every way to be generous in every way, which through us will produce thanksgiving to God,"
2 Corinthians 9:11 (NIV)

"Give thanks in all circumstances; for this is God's will for you in Christ Jesus,"
1 Thessalonians 5:18 (NIV)

20 Helpful Self-Assessment Questions before pursuing your "Dream Home" or "Dream Marriage"

1. What does your dream home look like?

2. Describe what an ideal marriage looks like? Name couples you consider as role models.

3. Describe your childhood home (physical characteristics, size, layout, etc.), who lived there and their relationship with you?

4. Think about your earliest recollections of home and describe what stands out as your happiest memories? Your most painful ones?

5. Which emotions do you associate most with your childhood home?

6. Who did you admire or feel most supported by growing up? Why?

7. What are your favorite rooms in any home and why?

8. When and where do I feel most like myself?

9. What are my "core values"? – Those fundamental beliefs, ideals or practices that guide your behavior and decision making. The things that matter to you the most.

10. Do your current behaviors and relationships reflect your core values?

11. How often do you compromise on the things that matter to you the most?

12. Describe your current or previous experience with budgets.

13. How often do you consider how much you can afford before making major purchases?

14. How often do you buy things on impulse?

15. Do you consider yourself spiritual, or a person of faith? If so, what is your statement of belief?

16. How would you describe yourself spiritually? (curious, beginner, growing, mature or not applicable)?

17. Describe what compatibility looks like to you? How compatible are you with your current or previous significant other(s), physically, emotionally, spiritually?

18. Describe your current goals (both short-term 1-2 years, and long-term 5+ years)

19. What are you holding on to that you need to let go of before achieving your goals?

20. What are you most grateful for?

A Prayer for your Dream Home

God, thank You for the provision that makes finding an ideal home possible. Please guide me to a residence that I can proudly call my own, one that instills a sense of peace, safety, security, acceptance, happiness, and joy. Help me create a welcoming environment with my loved ones, ensuring we have everything necessary to grow, prosper, and thrive according to Your purpose. Establish my home with Your presence, grant me wisdom, and surround me with Your love as I extend that love to everyone who enters. I appreciate Your faithfulness in all You have done and will do. Lastly, thank You for Your kindness and generosity towards all of us, believers and non-believers alike.

—Amen

A Prayer for Your Dream Marriage

God, thank you for creating marriage as part of your plan for humanity. I appreciate the bond where two can commit to each other and share love, companionship, and support. Help me understand the value healthy marriages bring to society, serving as a basis for a happy life and community. God, thank you for the security marriage offers, and help me see it as a reflection of Your relationship with Your people. Teach me to love unconditionally, communicate honestly, forgive sincerely, and sacrifice frequently in marriage. Strengthen my faith in marriage and in You.

-Amen.

About The Author

Alison Crews is a seasoned technology leader with over two decades of experience in leadership and technical roles across the Big Tech, Telecommunications, and Cybersecurity sectors. She has successfully led global teams spanning the United States, Latin America, Europe, and Asia, bringing a wealth of cross-cultural and strategic insight to her work.

In addition to her accomplished career in technology, Alison pursued her deep interest in mental health by earning a master's degree in counseling psychology. She has since dedicated her time and expertise to several nonprofit organizations, focusing on co-occurring disorders (addiction and mental health), crisis intervention, and hospice care.

Combining her professional experience and personal passion, Alison founded a Counseling Ministry within her local faith community, merging evidence-based mental health practices with spiritual principles.

She also established K.E.P.T., a Marriage Ministry that supports couples both within her church and in the broader community.

Alison is a sought-after speaker and teacher, known for her engaging and insightful talks on women's issues, youth and young adult development, healthy relationships, and emotional wellness. Her commitment to empowering individuals in their faith, careers, relationships, and mental health has inspired many.

Now adding "author" to her list of accomplishments, Alison is set to release her debut book, *The Big Reveal: Keys to Building Your Dream Home and Your Dream Marriage*, on May 15, 2025.

Connect with Author

🌐 TheBigRevealBook.com

✉ Alison@thebigrevealbook.com

in linkedin.com/in/alison-crews-5890b778/

▶ youtube.com/@thebigrevelbook

f facebook.com/@thebigrevealbook

www.ingramcontent.com/pod-product-compliance
Lightning Source LLC
Chambersburg PA
CBHW070405200326
41518CB00011B/2067